A NEW APPROACH TO APPLIED RESEARCH:
Race and Education

ELIZABETH G. COHEN
Stanford University

Charles E. Merrill Publishing Company
A Bell & Howell Company
Columbus, Ohio

International Standard Book Number: 0-675-09345-7

Library of Congress Catalog Card Number: 76-110779

1 2 3 4 5 6 7 8 9 10 — 75 74 73 72 71 70

Printed in the United States of America

To Dr. Howard B. Jefferson,
who introduced me to the importance
of analytic thinking

PREFACE

This approach to research is designed to benefit the different purposes of different members of the educational, and sociological audience: for the *practitioner*—research which provides general rules for applying a manipulation to his unique field situation, telling him what features of his situation are critical for successful repetition of the researcher's results; for the *policy maker*—research closely designed to provide answers to his questions; questions he could conceivably do something about; and for the *applied researcher* in education and sociology—a picture of the research process with a firm basis in the construction of a researchable set of propositions. The building material in these propositions is often borrowed from theoretical and empirical work already completed in basic behavioral science research. Testing these basic ideas may be done through either controlled analysis in surveys or experimentation. After a series of tests provide confidence in the projected manipulation of the basic propositions, there is a final engineering stage of clinical field testing. It is the contention of this book that beginning with an abstract formulation of the problem may yield newer ideas and more generally workable propositions than beginning with the common-sense categories of people who are working in the field.

Specifically, the book concerns questions of initial research formulation, analysis of the phenomenon and/or the problem to be studied, and the phrasing of the research question. There are many extended examples of original research designs which illustrate the style of formulation I am proposing. These examples are based upon the applied problems of race and education.

After several years of working as a sociologist with graduate students who are practitioners, administrators, researchers and future policy makers at the Stanford University School of Education, I am convinced that the basic researcher's approach provides a better understanding of many of the current questions. Much of the difficulty in producing useful social action research lies in the initial research formulation. Furthermore, these difficulties are typical of the published research available. This research could be more useful, powerful and practical than it is. If we would analyze the phenomenon and phrase the propositions for research in more selective and more abstract terms, we would know how to analyze and interpret the data. Many of the current formulations are too concrete and unsystematic. They are more like history than science; and they leave us at a loss when we wish to generalize to a new situation. If we could have the patience to test our basic propositions in a rigorous fashion and, carefully guided by clinical considerations, move into progressively more complex field situations, I believe practitioners would find research applications more useful and important than they are now.

The first two chapters of this book present a diagnosis of the present state of conceptualization in applied research. The difficulties faced by the practitioner and the policy maker in attempting to use current research are discussed.

The next three chapters analyze the famous "Coleman Report", *Equality of Educational Opportunity*, as research designed to meet the needs of governmental social policy. A new and alternative method for making diagnostic social surveys is described in detail. Also presented in a chapter co-authored by Bernard P. Cohen, is a special, controlled comparison survey method recommended for seeking answers to current policy questions, such as the effects of *de facto* segregation.

In the final three chapters, I cover the experimental approach; my research on the possible amelioration of interracial interaction problems is described in some detail. A new theoretical and research formulation of the minority group child's problem of powerlessness in the depressed area public elementary school is also proposed.

In writing, I have used the approach and examples that have proved successful in communicating with students not trained in sociology or research or the philosophy of science. In this way, I hope to reach many people in addition to those actively engaged in research, people who wish to keep up with and utilize the latest in educational research.

I would like to acknowledge the work of my husband, Bernard P. Cohen, in the philosophy of basic sociological research, which had a profound influence on my writing and thinking. I also would like to thank the students of the School of Education and my colleagues who have taught me so much about strategic problems in the field of race and education.

TABLE OF CONTENTS

one

THE DEMANDS ON EDUCATION

Prevent youngsters from dropping out before high school graduation by any and all means. Develop new curricula producing a generally educated and educable high school graduate who can adapt to future unknown changes in technology. Intervene in the life of the "culturally deprived child" so that unrelieved poverty will not pass from generation to generation. Correct the educational conditions, especially in the depressed area school, which have made school a punitive and failing experience for a large portion of the population. Change the school environment of the minority group child, allowing him to compete equally with the dominant majority throughout his life.

We ask the school to do all these things: to hold, motivate, and educate every child to a far higher level than was even dreamed of a few years ago. Not only are we asking the school to solve specific educational problems, but also we want to use education as a means for correcting pervasive social ills having roots in many other parts of society, such as poverty and discrimination.

CURING SOCIAL ILLS

Why should the school be the focus of the current drive to cure societal ills? The school has become virtually the only path to lifetime employability in the modern American occupational world. Correctly or not, we no longer assume that people can learn most white-collar jobs and many technical blue-collar jobs through informal apprenticeship situations. We insist upon the formal criteria of training, such as a high school diploma, a college degree, or completion of a training course, whether sponsored by public monies or by industry itself. Secondly, the school has become inextricably linked with the Civil Rights movement and has become the great hope of the Negro people in their drive to overcome discrimination and rise from the bottom of the socioeconomic heap. Lastly, education receives great attention because national and local policy makers view it as a more easily manipulable institution than other societal institutions. Many students and practitioners of public education in this country doubt the capacity of public education to undergo any serious social change in the direction desired, and they doubt the wisdom of abandoning purely educational goals in the schools for broader social goals. These are not popular viewpoints in today's era of educational panaceas, but they deserve serious consideration.

What a formidable task has been set for the public schools considering their serious financial problems and their observable slowness in accepting any major changes beyond the attachment of special programs which do not change the power structure. Consider the sheer lack of scientific or practical know-how for the accomplishment of these goals! Until recent pressures upon the schools, the aims for children with motivational problems, children with below average IQ scores, and children from culturally deprived homes were extremely limited. At its best, the school system provided kindly custodial care for these children, catering to their needs through "life adjustment" curricula and shop courses. At its worst, the school system punished them with constant low evaluations, informing them of their grave limitations as educable human beings.

EDUCATIONAL RESEARCH AS THE ANSWER

CONVENTIONAL PROFESSIONAL WISDOM

The response of the policy makers at the national level and in the field of professional education has been to turn to educational research and innovation (with or without research) for the answers to these problems. At first, ideas of what make really good schools, which had been in the field of education for some time, were practiced in certain depressed areas; ideas of better physical facilities, smaller classes, and more specialists. It was simpler to buy better schools than to part with any cherished assumptions concerning the universal applicability of currently held notions. Literature is beginning to show now discouragement with these initial attempts, although there is a conspicuous lack of satisfactory systematic evaluations.

Tannebaum eloquently phrases the difficulty with the simpler "educational panacea" solution:

> It was so easy and fashionable to believe that the educational ills of some children could be cured by providing them with modern school buildings, decent-sized classes, a rich variety of instructional equipment, lavish pupil personnel services and experienced teachers and principals—if only the facts supported the beliefs. Sadly, they do not. Learning conditions in many slum schools compare favorably with those in better neighborhoods; yet, learning and behavior problems remain critical among the lower status children who attend these schools . . . there has been entirely too much evangelism in the field and too little patient thinking and hardnosed research. Every so often we hear reformers excoriating the schools for their poor records in depressed areas and confidently suggesting solutions. Their well-meaning efforts often attract an enthusiastic following of hopeful educators in desperate need of help. The let-down comes later, when the jeremiad is ended, the dust clears, and the results are in. The bald fact is that we have not solved the problem as yet, nor do we have a fool-proof solution on the drawing board.[1]

INNOVATION VS. RESEARCH

There has been in the past year, an increase in the proliferation of concrete proposals and programs for schools serving culturally deprived and minority group children. We call these programs examples of educational innovation rather than research since they are not designed with the goal of scientific exploration or any systematic accumulation of knowledge in mind. Rather, they begin with someone's "gut conviction" that something will work. The initial conceptualization of the idea is in terms adapted from the administrator's, teacher's, or layman's vocabulary: "drop-out," "behavior problem," or "Negro." No particular connection is made between any known intellectual forebearers and the recommended technique. If there is any systematic evaluation, such as a control group (very infrequent because of the widespread conviction that no child should be deprived of the latest innovation), or a follow-up study, only the crudest measures, such as changes in IQ scores, are used. In an intellectual sense, these innovators have not isolated a phenomenon for discussion; they have no broad framework to explain their means

---

[1] Abraham Tannenbaum, "Curriculum Perspectives for Slum Schools," *The High School and the Big Cities: Conference Report,* ed. N. Boyan (Mimeo Conference Report, Stanford University, 1963), pp. 1-3.

and ends in anything other than operational terms. If their evaluation measures do show success, they cannot explain why they succeeded or under what conditions success might occur again.

In addition, we have witnessed vast support within and without the field of professional education for educational research of a behavioral science variety. The move toward the behavioral science as an academic source of concepts and methods of research has not occurred suddenly. For some time, major changes have been occurring in some graduate schools of education, laying the groundwork for reliance on both empirical research as a method of inquiry and psychology, sociology, and anthropology as sources of concepts and hypotheses.

The more influential graduate schools of education have moved closer to their universities' academic mainstream. The relationship between the behavioral sciences and the better schools of education has grown particularly close. With the growth of research speciality in educational psychology, we have a discipline oriented towards inquiry and devoted specifically to the greater understanding of educational phenomena. An upsurge of interest in the sociology of education as a sub-speciality of research oriented sociology has supplemented the deepening intellectual substance of the educational field. Similarly, in social anthropology, there are well-trained students of the school and society.

In the faculty, there are increasing joint appointments between schools of education and academic departments, of people who can qualify for either setting; this is particularly true of psychology. We now see academically trained individuals, who have never taught in the public schools, teaching their particular behavioral science discipline on the graduate level within schools of education, without translating or watering down the materials for the benefit of the students.

Parallel to these substantive changes in the field of education are the changes in advanced graduate training programs in education. Research has become so important that there are now Ph.D.'s in education who are purely research trained and inquiry oriented, and who may never have taught. They will serve as research directors for large school systems, in jobs connected with research for the federal government, or as college professors who combine teaching and research. Graduates also will serve in the field of applied educational research done by independent firms, an area of growing investment.

All these Ph.D. candidates are expected to do a research dissertation, and many of these dissertations involve the behavioral and social sciences. For example, a doctoral degree in educational administration at one of these schools frequently will result in a dissertation on organizational problems, written in the terms of organizational theorists, with elaborate statistical analyses of systematically collected data.

An examination of current education journals will reveal the close connection between the behavioral sciences and the graduate field of education. Many articles in these current journals use the same concepts, study designs, methods of data analysis, and statistical techniques that are used in articles by contemporary behavioral scientists. Just as in the behavioral science journals, education journals use experimental and control groups, questionnaires and interviews, factor analyses, analyses of variance, hypotheses, and "statistically significant results." An examination of the vocabulary will reveal that concepts such as "reinforcement," "delayed gratification pattern," and "sub-culture," are often borrowed directly from the behavioral sciences.

Given this growing relationship between the more influential graduate schools of education and the fields of psychology, social psychology, and sociology, when the demand came for knowledge about the culturally deprived and minority-group child's failing experience in the public school system, the practitioners and the policy makers turned to the behavioral sciences for answers. The extensive literature on social class and racial differences in learning ability, as well as the literature on class differences in personality variables and style of life were reviewed. Behavioral scientists were supported in projects designed to examine the effects of on-going desegregation in southern cities. Developmental psychologists were called in to design pre-school programs. Symposia composed of behavioral scientists and educators sprouted everywhere, and many of the resulting papers were published.

THE STATE OF THE LITERATURE

Now there is available a large body of literature on "education for the disadvantaged." Some of it describes various concrete programs that have been tried; some of it recommends new approaches to practice and teaching. Under the heading of behavioral science research, there are many new studies on social class and racial differences in speech and learning ability as well as studies on class differences in personality variables and style of life. Sociologists also have examined differences between middle class and lower class schools in terms of their facilities and educational outcomes.

This literature has not proved particularly useful for the practitioner or the policy maker for various reasons detailed below. Many would say that we have not found the key factors yet and that the passage of time, as knowledge accumulates, will yield the answer. I don't think so. It is my contention that the major problem is the failure to conceptualize and analyze the particular research question at hand. What we presently have is both not practical enough to be used and not intellectual enough to be grasped on the basis of generally applicable abstract ideas. In our attempt to solve social problems quickly, we have taken some unfortunate short-cuts to useful empirical wisdom.

This weakness *prevents* the accumulation of knowledge needed for useable answers. Basically, this is an optimistic book. I have not given up hope that many of the action research problems (defined in workable terms) are capable of solution. I think that behavioral science has the concepts and methodological capability to solve selected problems, given a stubborn tough persistence and a willingness to place the work on a sounder conceptual basis.

If the aim of the action researcher is to produce applicable knowledge, his work must be designed to culminate in a series of rules for the practitioner. The remainder of this chapter will examine the claim that much of the present research is impractical for the purposes of the practitioner and the policy maker. Beginning with the failure to produce rules in the work now available, we will try to reach an analysis of the role of abstraction in the research process. The first part, then, isolates the basic criticism of contemporary applied research. The latter part of the book attempts to provide some constructive suggestions: methods of analyzing the initial research problem; ways to design studies in order to achieve a more general understanding; and a model of the research process composed of successive studies designed to achieve statements of the proper conditions for application of a finding.

THE PLIGHT OF THE PRACTITIONER

The practitioners who serve as administrators, teachers, and educational specialists in minority groups have tried to use the available literature. Their complaints that the research is in no condition to be used are frequently dismissed as a lack of sophistication, but in reality their complaints are perfectly justified.

LACK OF NEW IDEAS

As they read the literature coming from all this frenetic research, paper-giving, and experimenting with new school programs, they are struck by the lack of new ideas. No matter where the researcher begins, in concrete programs or in social class correlates, the recommendations have a familiar ring: pre-school programs; in-service training for teachers in culturally deprived areas; more guidance workers; new types of interesting and challenging vocational education; and instructional techniques for young children employing concrete rewards.[2] The practitioner frequently remarks, "Why go through all that trouble? I could have suggested that at the beginning."

Perhaps the practitioners are naive about research, and the widely recognized recommendations finally are receiving the documentation that they deserve. Perhaps the problem is a simple one, and a little careful consideration will produce wide agreement on the solution. But these ideas are being tried; and the results appear very mixed. An alternative explanation for this similarity of solutions is that they are popular, commonsense remedies which are tacked on to the "final conclusion" section whether or not they are logically implied. A careful examination of the available research will, I believe, reveal no clear, tight logical connection between what is found in the research and the practical solution. There is a world of implicit and untested assumptions between the propositions in the research and the "Practical Recommendations" section.

WILL IT WORK FOR ME?

Secondly, practitioners complain that they are never told in the research where and when to apply the recommended solution. Will it work in all inner city schools, for all ethnic and minority groups, or for all age children? Even if they seem to have the same setting as described in the original research, it is bound to be different in countless ways. There is no way of telling which of these differences will be important and which will be immaterial. This complaint is not a result of the "unfortunately concrete" mind of the practitioner; he is conscientious and aware of possible deleterious consequences of tinkering with situations such as the relationship between races in the school. He wants to have some confidence before he begins a new program.

In scientific terms, the practitioners point to the total lack of a theoretical framework in the available research. Without a series of propositions explicitly naming the important conditions *under which we may expect the observed relationship between remedial technique*

---

[2] For an excellent overview of this literature, see Benjamin S. Bloom, Allison Davis, and Robert Hess, *Compensatory Education for Cultural Deprivation* (New York: Holt, Rinehart & Winston, Inc., 1965).

and improved behavior to hold, a potential user of the information cannot analyze his own setting when considering the use of the technique.

UNIMPRESSIVE EVALUATION

Finally, practitioners are not impressed by the measures of evaluation used in research, such as the standardized achievement tests or changes in IQ score. Here the practitioners and the researchers are in agreement; neither is happy with this state of affairs. People who are familiar with the problems in educating culturally deprived children will state that the children can improve considerably in their learning behavior without having their improvement accurately reflected in standardized achievement tests. We have begun to suspect that many black children particularly are handicapped in a test-taking situation which means that a test is an especially unsuitable measure of what they have learned. Test-taking, contrary to what many school personnel may believe, is *not* the basic goal of the educational process. Favorable outcomes of recommended procedures may have to be measured in entirely original fashion.

Another commonly used method of evaluation is change in the IQ score as a measure of improvement in the learning situation. Again the practitioner may complain that we have no certain idea what this change may mean. If a recommended technique aims to improve a specific learning disability, the IQ score, whatever it may measure, is far too crude to judge specifically whether or not our treatment had the intended effect. There are too many factors that can account for the change in IQ scores between two testings: change in the testing situation; unreliability of the test; improvement in attitude toward test-taking; improvement in motivation toward learning; development of learning abilities etc. Furthermore, the score itself does not show where the child stands on specific abilities directly related to learning in school.

The problem is again one of conceptualization. If the researcher had isolated a phenomenon and abstracted the aspects he wished to deal with or had constructed some propositions concerning the relationship between the phenomenon and his recommended technique, he would never be in the awkward position of having to use crude and indirect evaluation techniques. Since he would know which learning disability he wishes to alter and have an idea of why it changes under the influence of his techniques, he would devise a direct test for change in that learning disability. As long as we talk about "problems of Negro children in school" and "problems of culturally deprived children in school" in relation to a broadly conceived program, we will never know where to look for evaluation purposes. In a real sense, we don't know what we are talking about.

THE PLIGHT OF THE POLICY MAKER

THE COST OF BEING WRONG

If the practitioners have problems with the available research, they are nothing compared to the problem of a policy maker. He has the same complaints as the practitioner and one additional headache: if he decides to recommend widespread support of a particular recommendation, he may make an expensive mistake. If he relies upon research based on a successful demonstration of a relationship, and it does not work in other settings, or it has unfortunate side-effects in some settings, the criticism and disillusionment of society is frightening to contemplate.

With considerable money at his disposal, the policy maker may institute vast programs because, seemingly, society is willing for him to solve these problems. But if policy is to be based on research (which is often not the case), he needs to have considerable confidence in the research. It doesn't seem sufficient to believe the author's word that a given correlation between the recommended technique and the child's improvement is due to the factors the researcher thinks it is. The policy maker needs a more substantial form of reassurance.

PRE-SCHOOL PROGRAM RESEARCH

An excellent example of this problem is the studies of children attending a pre-school program who appear to be superior to children not attending the pre-school program. The interpretation must show what in the pre-school program produced the improvement in the children's behavior. Was it really due to the specific techniques involved in the program? If so, was it one of them especially or all of them at once? It would be foolish to invest in two dozen techniques when one technique does all the work. Are some techniques good for some learning handicaps but harmful for other learning handicaps? Perhaps the positive result originates in the way the children were selected for the program. Perhaps interested parents came down and enrolled their children who were not really handicapped children in the first place. It may even be true, that the positive results are only a function of the increased attention paid to the children in the program causing them to feel that they are valued members of society. Surely, the policy maker deserves some answers to these questions before making a major commitment of funds.

SCIENCE AND TIME FOR THOUGHT

When research is not conceptualized properly, no amount of data or statistics will provide the answers for these important questions. If we want answers of this calibre for the policy maker and the practitioner, we must return to the beginning and examine the origin of our research categories and propositions. We cannot share the benefits demonstrated by applied physical science without better using the scientific method from the start. Although available research has many of the accouterments of science, it fails to meet certain criteria.

The hope is always present that with the accumulation of more research we will progress beyond the obvious solution, the evaluation problems, the difficulties of applying the research, and the uncertainty of the interpretations of the results. There is hope that we will progress to the gradual discovery of basic principles accounting for the educational maladjustment, thereby deriving proper solutions. But the difficulties with the available research are not just the early stages of scientific explanation: they are symptoms of a basic approach to research which has only the most superficial resemblance to accepted scientific models. There is no way for this approach to develop into the more explanatory, more theoretically oriented level needed by the practitioner and the policy maker.

The difficulty lies in the initial conceptualization of the problem; this stage of research has the most profound consequences for the usefulness of the research output. Considerable time and resources should be invested in the initial "thinking" phase of the research. We take the perennially painful and unpopular view of asking people already under pressure for immediate solutions to allow the researcher time to consider what he wants to abstract from the concrete practical problem and what testable propositions would describe the dynamic of this abstract version. In a seemingly illogical way, we claim the quickest way to solve practical problems through research will be to retreat temporarily to a neater, more abstract mode for the purpose of understanding some features of the problem.

In the following chapter we will analyze the problem of abstraction and explanation in applied research. Through concrete examples of common types of applied research, we will try to illustrate why the present mode is such a radical departure from the strength of the scientific approach.

Each chapter is an extended illustration of the style of conceptualization and research we are recommending. These research projects have a mode of arriving at concepts for research, a style for asking the question which can be researched, and an attempt to construct some systematic and/or theoretical basis for each testable proposition. The illustrations are designed to show how new ideas may follow from abstract conceptual approaches. Each of these chapters represents a different attempt to solve the research problems presented in these first two chapters, but they are all selected as a closer approach to normal scientific activity than much of the presently available research.

two

SCIENCE: A SPECIAL KIND
OF ABSTRACTION

Applied or action research only needs to differ from basic research in its insistence on dealing with a *particular* phenomenon. Since applied research begins with a problem focus, the investigator can use the scientific method as an aid to learning about the sources of a problem or the successful manipulation of the problem situation. He would do well to lean on all the strengths that the scientific method offers, including the use of scientific abstractions, propositions and sets of propositions.

Instead of concentrating on a particular phenomenon, the researcher views the *development of theory* as his major task. He may select a wide range of phenomena because they constitute critical tests of his key ideas. In other words, the basic researcher is *unrestricted* in the phenomena he will study as long as they constitute an instance of his theory. He is *restricted* to the system of abstract ideas he has chosen to study. The applied researcher is *restricted* as to the phenomenon he wants to study, but *unrestricted* as to the selection of abstract ideas, providing that they appear useful in understanding his problem.

NON-SCIENTIFIC FEATURES OF
CURRENT RESEARCH

At the moment, applied educational research bears many superficial resemblances to basic research in the behavioral sciences. They both use hypotheses; they both may use conventional design features such as experimental and control groups; and they both use statistical analyses of the data. There are two major fundamental differences between much of the applied research and basic research which are not *necessary* because of the nature of the applied research, as we have defined it. If these differences were to be erased, the research would still be pertinent to the problem at hand, but the message would be more powerful.

INITIAL CHOICE OF CONCEPTS

The first of these differences is the initial choice of concepts. The basic researcher will either choose or invent abstractions for constructing a parsimonious explanation of a group of events. For example, he will consider learning in terms of reinforcement theory, hoping to develop that theory as an explanation of many different events. The applied researcher in education typically *uses basic concepts from the people who are concerned with the immediate social problem*, i.e., the practitioner or the administrator. For example, he will use as research concepts terms such as "drop-out" or "behavior problem." He does not concern himself with the conceptual clarity of this initial choice or the excess meanings that later may burden his thinking; nor does he worry about any very complex system of explanation. He doesn't want to be involved in a complex process of reasoning because he has no time to lose.

USE OF SYSTEMATIC PROPOSITIONS

Secondly, the basic researcher in behavioral science usually tries to derive his propositions systematically from the intellectual antecedents of his abstractions. He tries to move carefully from what is known to what is unknown in such a manner that scientific knowledge will hopefully accumulate in some systematic way. He has very difficult problems using this hypothetico-deductive scientific method because he seldom uses mathematics or formal logic as a tool for unambiguous derivation. He tries to use a rougher, more informal logic, but he carefully states his implicit assumptions, his basic theoretical definitions and all the hypotheses that he can derive from this framework.

The applied researcher in education may borrow from the substance of the behavioral science the rough idea of a hypothesis, but he will substitute his own rough concepts as he adapts the hypothesis. Furthermore, he usually thinks it unnecessary to use more than the germ of the hypothesis itself. The hypothesis then is translated into operational terms. There is typically only one proposition at a time to test; and if there are two, they are not systematically related to each other. In other words, the applied researcher in education makes no serious attempt to select and borrow from the strengths of the work done in behavioral science. He sees no particular advantage in "hitching" onto some of the more highly developed sets of propositions such as those in the field of learning theory or attitude change.

With the choice of concepts and a hypothesis, probably involving not too much research time and personnel, the project starts with the intricacies of data collection. Since the theoretical definitions are sketchy if not absent, there is no particular way to decide how to collect data. Therefore, the researchers combine expediency, conventional practices, and a strategy of collecting extra masses of data, hoping that the truth will emerge out of all these facts.

In their attempt to be practical and solution-oriented, educational researchers ignore the essential initial phase of conceptualization in scientific work. Yet, this omission is not necessary since their research loses strength without it. At the heart of the scientific method lies abstraction. Scientists do not conceive of themselves as capturing concrete truth. Nor do they typically use an inductive method to cull truth from masses of facts.

The strength and success of the physical sciences, in particular, has lain in the use of hypothetico-deductive models employing abstractions. The scientist deals with only one part of any concrete phenomenon. He decides what class of events this particular phenomenon will be considered an instance of—the very act of abstraction.

PHYSICAL VS. BEHAVIORAL SCIENCES

In the very successful physical sciences, the choice of abstraction may not be problematic. It is usually dictated by some strikingly successful example of accepted scientific practice, whether a brilliant form of experiment or a fully developed hypothetico-deductive model. Kuhn refers to these models of scientific emulation as "paradigms;" and the physical scientist usually is found working within this accepted framework which is known to be successful.

> Normal science is, then, like a mop-up operation. Normally scientists do not invent new theories but attempt to articulate old ones. By focusing attention upon a small range of relatively esoteric problems, the paradigm forces scientists to investigate some part of nature in a detail and depth that would not otherwise be imaginable.[1]

---

[1] Thomas S. Kuhn, *The Structure of Scientific Revolution* (Chicago, Ill.: University of Chicago Press, 1962), p. 23.

The behavioral scientist, doing basic research, does not have widely accepted paradigms to emulate. He often has to create his own abstractions and almost certainly his own testable propositions. He is at a more primitive stage of scientific development. Nonetheless, he still follows the basic steps of abstracting the concrete phenomenon, viewing it as an instance of a more abstract class.

There is no reason why the applied researcher, interested in social action, cannot do the same thing. He can choose to view a given schoolroom phenomenon as an instance of reinforcement or alternatively, as an instance of the operation of status characteristics. Having selected a set of abstractions from the behavioral sciences which to him seem strategic, he can utilize what is known to formulate his assumptions and testable propositions. He may test these propositions in a field setting, in an experimental laboratory or through correlation in a controlled comparison. He is still an applied researcher because he is interested only in one type of phenomenon and not interested in testing the reinforcement theory or status characteristic theory on a very different type of phenomenon.

Let us turn now to a systematic examination of what the applied researcher gains from making his conceptualization like that in basic research in the behavioral sciences. Through a series of extended examples, the rest of this chapter will demonstrate the relationship between the two initial steps and the practicality of research. These steps are: the manner in which initial abstractions are made; and the presence or absence of a set of propositions stating the conditions under which a relationship holds. These initial steps, it will be argued, determine whether or not the final result is phrased in a manner allowing the practitioner to know where to apply the research. These initial steps also are related to the connection between the suggestion for improving the situation and the research: does it follow along directly or is it added after an intellectual gap? Finally, these initial steps help to provide a means of evaluating the technique proposed.

LACK OF CONCERN WITH THE UNIQUE EVENT

HISTORY VS. SCIENCE

The first problem in the abstraction employed in current work is the confusion of the historical with the scientific mode of viewing the world. Unlike the basic science people, both the applied researcher and the historian are particularly interested in certain concrete events. The historian wants to explain why a particular event in time and space happened. To make this explanation, he may borrow propositions from the sciences or economics or sociology, but his goal still is to explain why a given event took place. In contrast, the applied researcher in the physical sciences sees his unique event as one of a class of events and then proceeds to deal with propositions governing these classes of events.[2]

EXAMPLE: STUDIES OF DESEGREGATION

A concrete example taken from the field of applied educational research, of a project with an historical rather than a scientific approach would be a study of desegregation in particular cities. Here, the major argument concerns the resistances to desegregation in a particular city and at a particular time. Also, the researcher, in this case would try to discover why the city still has not completely desegregated.

It is quite possible to study desegregation from a more scientific point of view. But the first step the researcher must take if he is to draw closer to the successful model of applied physical sciences is to decide just what type of a phenomenon desegregation is, and what body of available conceptualization in the behavioral sciences is most appropriate for the examination of the problem. The most cursory review of available concepts in the behavioral sciences would demonstrate that it is not easy to decide which concepts best characterize desegregation. Desegregation is tied to American history at this particular juncture. However, one could decide that he is really interested in the effects of desegregation on white children. Does it really make them less prejudiced? A frequently used proposition in the social science literature is that equal status contact will produce a reduction in racial or religious prejudice.

We are then forced to take the next step in discovering the extent that desegregation actually represents equal status contact. We might find that some instances of desegregation, because of the manner in which it is done, more nearly resemble the condition called "equal status contact" than other instances. This example demonstrates how the process of deciding consciously upon the method of abstracting a given class of events, will result in different operations on the data, different studies and eventually different solutions. Compare the recommendations the researcher makes if he begins in historical terms to study desegregation in schools of various cities with recommendations derived from scientifically

---

[2] For a thorough discussion of this distinction between scientific and historical methods see Karl R. Popper, *Poverty of Historicism* (New York: Harper & Row, 1964), pp. 143-44.

oriented applied research. Unless he makes the abstraction, all he can do is state that City A is different from City B because of a series of geographical or economic or what-have-you factors. What does he gain from this comparison between cities in the way of recommendations for creating a more rapid and effective desegregation process? His recommendation will be only indirectly related to his comparison of the cities. On the other hand, if he narrows his problem to an instance of the desired effect of desegregation he quickly realizes which instances represent equal status contact. If these instances are correlated with a lessening of white children's prejudice, he can recommend certain steps. In other words, he can suggest that schools which have not made desegregation an instance of equal status contact take steps to more closely approximate this model.

This extended example not only demonstrates the difference in the approach of the scientifically oriented applied researcher as compared to the historically oriented applied researcher, but also emphasizes that, although we do not have successful paradigms in basic behavioral sciences as guidelines, we can use a model of successful science in the following ways: a self-conscious utilization of abstraction; and the construction of a set of logically interrelated propositions whenever possible. If we are able to construct a set of logically interrelated propositions, we will characterize more effectively the dynamic of the phenomenon we are studying.

THE FAILURE TO ABSTRACT

If we wish to study the operation of a recommended technique, it is better not to state the problem in the original administrative terms. Let us use as an example the study of the Higher Horizons program which was based on a belief of the helpfulness of increased guidance services.

The practitioners involved in the program did not develop an idea of what the guidance services were supposed to do for youngsters on a more abstract level than the one used by the practitioner. As a result, the evaluation is quite puzzling. The initial program showed good success, but when expanded to include many more students, the success rate dropped. What went wrong? This example comprises failure to abstract from a concrete event; that is, a specific program with a specific professional approach. How do we know what essential elements must not be economized upon when the program is expanded?

We must have a more systematic way of understanding what this type of guidance program does in developing an individual, given certain characteristics of that individual and certain characteristics of his inter-action with the school personnel. The actual phenomenon of the guidance process can be conceptualized in several different directions. There are some interesting conceptualizations in terms of reinforcement theory, and some interesting attempts to characterize it as essentially a process of attitude change. The researcher has some choice, depending upon what system of concepts he can use most easily. But it is important for him, when he wishes to study a concrete program such as Higher Horizons, to decide which aspects of the guidance process are most relevant to the hoped for behavioral changes. Having made this decision, he can then characterize how the initial Higher Horizons program func-tioned in respect to particular aspects of the guidance process.

Then he is in a better position to analyze what the important changes in variables were when the program was enlarged. He is in a better position to say where the program should or should not be altered when the number of students involved is changed. Putting this in propositional form, to enlarge the program, the researcher must have a sufficient understanding of the variable to ask: Given a tremendous increase in the number of people being processed, what essential elements must remain unchanged if we are to achieve the same degree of results as we did with a much smaller number of students?

USING JUST ONE ABSTRACTION

COMPARING POPULATIONS

The next example is typical of much applied education research. There is abundant literature which compares socially disadvantaged children with less disadvantaged children on any one of a number of characteristics. There is usually a hypothesis which predicts that socially disadvantaged children have more or less "X" than less socially disadvantaged children. Having found an association between social disadvantage and the ab-sence of the characteristic, the authors usually make some suggestions for improving the situation. There is, in this research, certainly a process of abstraction; the idea of choosing a social class difference and one from the many characteristics that make up cultural deprivation is a form of abstraction involving concepts borrowed from the behavioral sciences. Although abstraction from the practitioner's operations level is involved, these studies really are not attached to any systematic bodies of concepts from behavioral science. They are more or less disembodied comparisons.

Summarizing the many research articles of this particular style, Edmund Gordon[3] points to differences that have been found in language, cognition, intelligence, perceptual styles, patterns of intellectual function, and motivation and aspiration. For example, according to a study cited by Gordon on environment and intelligence by Boyd McCandless,[4] the socially disadvantaged child tended to be more concrete and inflexible in his intellectual functioning than did the more privileged child.

A WEAK SOURCE OF RECOMMENDATIONS

The difficulty with this type of study becomes apparent when the researcher attempts to make some recommendation. When he attempts to recommend a technique for socially disadvantaged children to, let us say, increase the flexibility of their thinking, he can make almost an infinite number of suggestions. In other words, his original comparison between status groups told him nothing of how the thinking process became inflexible and in what circumstances it can be changed. Must interference with the growth of inflexible thinking take place at an early age, or can we attempt to change it at the high school age? Is it too late? We have no way of telling if the inflexible thinking is a basic factor or merely a superficial symptom. If it is merely a superficial symptom and we manage to remove it through a recommended technique, we still will have the basic disability in learning even though we have decreased the incidence of a particular symptom.

WHO NEEDS WHAT HELP?

The second basic difficulty with this style of research is that although one has a significant difference in the instance of a given characteristic between the two status populations, one cannot necessarily conclude that every socially disadvantaged child one meets shares this characteristic "X." And if every socially disadvantaged child does not share characteristic "X," then a massive recommended technique which involves a basic curriculum change for, let us say, the early grades may be quite inappropriate. This example demonstrates the need for more conceptual structure in order to move from the research design to a remedial suggestion and to identify and correct learning problems in certain socially disadvantaged children.

---

[3] Edmund Gordon, "Characteristics of Socially Disadvantaged Children," *The Review of Educational Research*, XXXV, No. 5 (1965), 377-78.
[4] *Ibid.*, p. 379.

The difficulty with research designed to document differences between populations is well described by Gordon in the conclusion of his article:

> Our efforts at documenting the characteristics have not identified the cause nor have they pointed clearly toward the courses of remediation.[5]

It remains for research to determine the nature of the learning facility and disability in this population; to determine those circumstances under which certain characteristics and conditions result in success and under which other characteristics and conditions result in failure; to develop more sensitive and accurate procedures to assess the potential for development as well as for behavioral change; and to determine those conditions where existing pedagogical principles and technology are inappropriate to the learning experience. This is required for a wide variety of underdeveloped learners.

In review, the example of Higher Horizons was a case of total failure to abstract from the typical functioning of the school system. We tried to show that without this abstraction we were unable to evaluate or to make predictions concerning any changes in the treatment. A second example involved an abstraction of at least one level. A concept borrowed from the behavioral sciences was selected and its incidence in two populations, a relatively advantaged and a relatively disadvantaged population, was compared. Difficulty in the second example arose despite the fact there was one level of abstraction because only a single concept was borrowed and was not imbedded in a propositional structure. There was no statement attempting to explain why one of the populations differed from the other. In other words, there was no attempt to capture the dynamic of the phenomenon. The lack of such a conceptualization produced an intellectual gap between the initial research findings and any conceivable suggestions for manipulating the phenomenon. Borrowing a single concept and utilizing a study design which is only constructed to compare the probability of a given characteristic are not suitable for generating suggestions.

The failure to use abstractions and propositions which are available or develop new propositions, accounts, in great part, for the impracticality of much available applied research. Without a set of conditions to explain to the potential user what he will need to have or create in order to experience the success of some previous innovator, he has no way to know whether someone's idea is transferable. The set of conditions must be abstractly phrased, as a set of ground rules for the operation of

---

[5] *Ibid.,* p. 385.

the ameliorative action. In addition, if the user can grasp the essence of the explanation for the success, in both general and abstract terms, he can apply the idea to a setting which differs in many external features from the original. Yet, he may have some confidence that he will also achieve success. Research which simply tinkers with concrete programs and refuses to abstract does not provide the critical information necessary to analyze the practitioner's own situation. It does not tell him the key elements to include in his program. Research which makes no attempt to explain, in abstract terms, how a disability comes about or how the disability functions, cannot logically recommend a way to remove the disability. Thus we have called much of the available research, "impractical."

three
SCIENTIFIC SOCIAL POLICY: FACT OR FICTION

The attention social scientists have received from policy makers in Washington who are concerned with the Civil Rights Revolution has been very flattering. Ever since their testimony in the Supreme Court desegregation decision, there has been a growing conviction that social science evidence can be used to find solutions to the social and economic problems surrounding the relationship between blacks and whites. For some time now, funding agencies of the government have supported university research on these problems; and many social scientists are working as part of permanent government staff. Two recent uses of social science evidence signal an even closer relationship between social policy decision making and the behavioral scientist. These are the reports, *Equality of Educational Opportunity* (usually referred to as the Coleman Report)[1] commissioned by Congress, and the Moynihan Report[2] on the Negro family, completed by Moynihan when he was a Presidential adviser.

Although these are both correlational studies, the Coleman Report is based on an ambitious national survey, while the Moynihan Report is an analysis of already collected data. Both these reports are resulting in a

---

[1] James S. Coleman, Ernest Q. Campbell, Carl J. Hobson, Alexander M. Mood, Frederic D. Weinfeld, and Robert L. York, *Equality of Educational Opportunity,* U.S. Department of Health, Education and Welfare, U.S. Office of Education (Washington, D.C.: Government Printing Office, 1966).

[2] Daniel Patrick Moynihan, "The Negro Family: The Case for National Action," in *The Moynihan Report and the Politics of Controversy,* Lee Rainwater and William L. Yancey (Cambridge, Mass.: The M.I.T. Press, 1967), pp. 39-124.

stormy history of controversy: both policy makers and pressure groups find in the data almost whatever they care to find. The authors of the Coleman Report, in particular, were quite careful to define the limitations of the survey; but these limitations have not stopped people who read the correlations for themselves or even worse, people who read what others say about the survey's implications. Such events are enough to make a reputable social scientist sorry he ever helped Washington.

THE UNACHIEVED IDEAL

We have yet to see a social policy truly based on research, which may surprise the readers of pseudo-scientific solutions to social problems. Unfortunately, the science of these solutions is not in a form to generate recommendations. The science becomes more symbolic than real; and the social scientist finds his research results utilized for political ends in ways he feels are illegitimate.

In the next four chapters we would like to attempt an answer to a pair of vital questions: How can the social scientist protect himself from dangerous misinterpretations of his data by policy makers and pressure groups; and what can the social scientist do to design research which will constitute a stronger basis for policy formation? In this first chapter we will consider the social scientist's and policy maker's differences and difficulties. They obviously have very different ways of viewing the world although they may share the same concerns about social problems. Assuming people really wanted to use social science to its greatest advantage (and it is not clear that everyone does) what kind of a research process would best utilize the scientist's available tools? We shall outline such a process in this chapter.

The second chapter discusses in greater detail the particular problems of the descriptive stage of the research process where the goal is to estimate the frequency and intensity of a social problem. The Coleman Report will be used to emphasize the differences between the traditional approach to a descriptive survey and the approach recommended in these chapters. The third chapter will examine the research requirements for confidence in the quality of a proposed manipulation of the social situation by the government or another social agency. Again, a contrast will be made between the traditional method of employing a survey for explanatory purposes and the recommended method which involves the use of a theory, research designs capable of coping with explanation, and experimental field testing. The last chapter will discuss the problem of estimating effects of altering racial composition of the schools as a special case of survey technique designed to handle a current policy question.

VALUE JUDGMENTS

Returning to the underlying motivations for constructing social policy propositions, let us first analyze the language used by the policy maker in dealing with social problems. Very often, it seems, he begins with an unvarnished value judgment for there is a reasonable political tradition of remaining nonempirical during the formulation of a policy.

The policy maker may, if he wishes, act almost solely on the *belief* that the actual state of affairs is "bad." When Civil Rights groups, as representatives of minority groups, state that minority group children receive a second-class education which damages their chances for acquiring the good things in life, the policy maker may decide that some steps should be taken. He hopes to convince the minority groups that they are no longer second-class citizens. In a society of equals, it goes without saying that no significant proportion of the population should feel like second class citizens. Furthermore, the feeling of inequality in education conflicts with two other cherished American ideals: belief in mass education and belief in the school as an equalizer of accidents such as coming from a poor family. If Civil Rights groups and other liberal elements in society select de facto segregation of northern schools as the symbol of second class citizenship and strive for its removal, the policy maker may try to comply without consulting a social scientist except possibly for technical aid on implementing such a policy. If he changes the minority group's belief, he has, from a policy point of view, taken a real step forward.

The form of the value statements commonly used by the policy maker is not suitable for empirical testing. For example: "there should be equality of opportunity for all Americans" is simply a statement of a desired end or goal. These statements of ends or value judgments, if properly formulated and operationalized, do become empirically testable propositions and questions. If we know what to look for, we can discover whether the observed state of affairs approximates an "equality of opportunity" model. If we know what the policy maker would like to do to achieve equality of opportunity, we have a means-end statement that can be researched. Do the free public schools actually accomplish equality of opportunity? Do the preferred means accomplish the preferred goal? Because we operate in an area of widely shared social preferences does not mean that decisions can only be made on purely ideological grounds.[3]

WHAT IS THE EVIDENCE OF THE PROBLEM?

The policy maker wishes to alert those people in charge of resources to a social problem. The failure of minority groups to use schools as ladders to upward mobility is a political and ethical affront. But he must demonstrate that the problem is sufficiently severe and/or extensive to necessitate the investment of social resources. In other words, the policy maker needs some evidence on "just how bad the situation is."

It is a great mistake for the social scientist, called to the aid of the policy maker at this juncture, to collect data on the problem in the form of the policy maker's commonsense categories without first examining the consequences of these categories for research. We recommend a distinct departure from the general practice of the surveyor called in to study a social problem. For example, the Coleman Report appeared to proceed on this basis when it hurried to execute the mammoth survey task under a provision of the Civil Rights Act of 1964 for the Commissioner of Education. Data were gathered from nearly 4,000 public schools on students in grades 1, 3, 6, 9 and 12.[4] Variables included an incredible range both in levels of abstraction and in sources, (from questionnaires on an individual's attitudes, to school district expenditure figures, to standardized test results, to school officials' estimates on characteristics of their schools).

The official government report could only partially analyze the overwhelming amount of data, and, at this writing, many analysts still are working with the data on tapes inside and outside government offices. It is almost as if with the advances in computer processing of data, the investigators attempted to photograph and capture the "realities" of the contemporary educational scene. This is the work of the historian rather than the scientist. Furthermore, if the applied research is seen initially in terms of all the variables the clients imagine to be relevant, it allows the policy maker to interpret the resulting data as he wishes.

The policy maker needs to have an estimate of the extensity and intensity of what is defined as a "social problem." In our terms, he needs

---

[3] This position may be characterized philosophically as an experimentalist view of values. We are indebted to L. Thomas for his assistance on this point: "Prospects of Scientific Research Into Values," *Educational Theory*, 1956, 6:193-214 (Converting value judgments into factual propositions which can be empirically tested).
[4] Coleman, *Equality of Educational Opportunity*, p. 8.

a series of empirical generalizations concerning the observable departures of current American society from the ideal value. For example, do minority groups in America today lack the educational opportunities that are available to the majority group? Is there discrimination on the basis of race in the hiring practices of industry?

PHENOMENAL VALUE MODELS

The researcher must first discover what the value judgments of the policy maker involve. How can he study the fulfillment of a value if a value judgment is not directly observable? Basically, he must decide what the social value *will look like* if it is fulfilled, or if the observable falls far short of the ideal.

TRANSLATION INTO OBSERVABLES

First, what observable phenomena will we label as instances of "equality of opportunity"? When researchers and policy makers analyze the phrase, "equality of opportunity," at least two phenomena come to mind. For one policy maker, the key social variable is variation in school facilities. Only if variation in school facilities is totally uncorrelated with racial composition of schools, will he be satisfied that the value is fulfilled. For another policy maker, the concentration on facilities for the *phenomenal model* will not be at all satisfactory; he is more interested in educational outcomes. Unless the researcher can show that black and white children derive equal learning from an equal number of years in school, he will continue to feel we have a severe social problem. The researcher must develop alternative phenomenal models to explicate the value judgment in ways that will satisfy the questions of both policy makers.

Turning to a value from the field of professional educators, suppose the researcher is asked to study whether or not classroom teachers are sensitive to individual needs. To study this question, he may observe several different phenomena in a classroom: variation of the instructional strategy according to some rationale based upon individual differences; or variation in emotional support and reinforcement given to each child according to some rationale based upon emotional needs. These two different phenomena (there may be others) require very different sets of operations for actual study. Clients may be surprised to learn that teachers who do one of the things fairly well, may not do the other at all well.

EMPIRICAL CRITERION STATEMENTS

Secondly, in his series of conferences with the policy maker, the researcher must discover which set of empirical results would cause the client to feel that "things are as they should be" or that things are as they "ought not to be."

In more abstract language, he translates the initial value statement to a *phenomenal* level where he explicates the observable features of the social scene which are considered pertinent. When the nature of these observables has been agreed upon, the construction of a series of *empirical criterion statements* begins for the purpose of interpreting the survey's results. The researcher and policy maker consider the potential findings on the state of these observables; they decide ahead of time, which pattern of findings will cause the conclusion that the observed state constitutes a departure from the ideal state of affairs. It is agreed that all other conceivable results will not be labeled a violation of the ideal state. The phenomena chosen for study with the set of empirical criterion statements constitute what we have called the *phenomenal model*.

Still, beyond the task of conceptualization, is the job of sample design and the selection of indicators to measure the social phenomena. The policy maker at a federal level typically will want results on the phenomenal model for different regions of the country. In the case of the Coleman Report, the Congress wanted some information on specific minority groups in different regions.

After the data are collected, analyzed, and the pattern of results evaluated according to the pre-arranged plan, the empirical generalizations and the judgments on departures from ideal states of the phenomenal models, are returned to the policy makers. It should be clearly understood that the results represent observations compared to expected outcomes on one of several phenomenal abstract models and are not a sample of concrete reality.

After the policy maker has the results of the descriptive survey, i.e., the judgments on observation in terms of several phenomenal models, he should find it easier to judge which particular type of improvement he wants. He can judge which model should have priority on one of the following bases: one model's observable consequences will violate the ideal state in many areas of the country; or the observable consequences of one model will indicate a rather straightforward political solution with a high probability of visible short-range improvement; or the sheer process of analysis will show the policy maker that he feels more strongly about one of these phenomenal models than another.

PROPOSITIONS FOR POLICY

In this ideal version of policy formulation, no one mentions social solutions until the results of the descriptive phase are in. Until the nature of the problem is formulated, it is impossible to suggest solutions within a scientific frame of reference. Of course, the researcher is not the only source of suggested solutions; there may be a wide interest in one particular recommendation such as school desegration; or the policy maker may see a powerful but purely political solution to one phenomenal value model.

SURVEYS AS A SOURCE OF HYPOTHESES

The researcher seeks a potential explanation of the phenomenon he describes in his initial survey. As soon as he decides that the observed phenomenon sharply differs from the expected, he speculates on potential causes for this state of affairs. Crude hypotheses are constructed during the analysis of the data, and if the relevant indicators of hypothesized antecedent variables have been included, the investigator will do some correlational analyses. These correlational analyses are between potential antecedent variables and the consequent variation in the observables of the social problem. For example, when Coleman examines the substandard performance rate of children attending depressed area schools, he hypothesizes that this might be an instance of "contextual effect" often studied by sociologists. The contextual effect is the social context of the situation which is believed to effect the individual over and above the individual characteristics that are brought to the situation. In his correlational analysis, Coleman attempts to hold constant certain characteristics of the school and the individual while varying the social class composition to discover if it will predict the individual's performance.[5] If he finds a positive correlation between social class composition of the school and the performance of the individual of a given social class attending a school with certain facilities, he has *begun* to identify a predictor variable. In effect, he tells us that "social class composition of the school predicts performance rate."

We need to construct a more powerful statement for an ideal policy proposition, one using something similar to the following form: if we vary x, then certain predictable changes will occur in y. The reader should make no mistake—this powerful type of proposition requires far more evidence than the merely observed association between two vari-

---

[5] Coleman, *Equality of Educational Opportunity,* pp. 302-10.

ables. This proposition requires no less than an *effective understanding of how the two variables come to be associated*. In terms of the social context explanation introduced above, the observed association is not sufficient assurance for manipulating the social composition of schools (or the racial composition of schools) for the purpose of improving the performance of low status (or minority group) children.

A SERIES OF STUDIES

Social manipulation typically involves major financial and political costs. It is bound to make many voters unhappy. Therefore, the policy maker requires a fair degree of confidence that the manipulation will be effective before he commits himself. The only way social scientists can give him this confidence is through the development of some theories on how the predictor variable is associated with the dependent variable.

If we formulate some ideas of the processes involved, we must move to some explicitly designed studies testing the power of our explanatory ideas. Very likely, these studies will be conducted under highly controlled conditions which will allow us to use a pure version of the major variables. Equally important, the design of these studies would allow us to examine several testable consequences of our process notions, not just the dependent variable which is our target for reform. After testing our first ideas of explanatory processes with suitable research designs, we may need to alter those ideas and test again. We will repeat this procedure until the data reliably fit explanatory propositions and *a priori* hypotheses. The research process is similar to a set of successive approximations in which we alter ideas to fit data and then generate new data to test the altered ideas.

ENGINEERING RESEARCH

Having studied the possibilities of manipulating one variable to obtain the desired change in another variable in a relatively controlled setting, we need assurance that we will get similar results in the less controlled world. Perhaps the operation of variables in the field situation will drastically alter the process we have been manipulating. Perhaps there are serious unanticipated and deleterious consequences of the proposed problem solution.

Before a policy solution is implemented, we need extensive field experiments. We need to check all the same points as the more controlled studies to discover whether or not the explanation continues to predict relationships between variables in the field. Highly skilled clinicians are required at this stage for their judgments of possible harm to organizations and individuals involved. No doubt, some tinkering with the concrete details of the operation will occur at this stage.

What a difference, however, between tinkering in this situation, and fiddling with someone's bright idea which has not come through a previous research process! Having some set ideas of the situation's key features which are designed to improve the problem, we know which things may be arranged to suit a particular clinical problem. We also know which things must not be altered if we don't want to change the basic effective conditions for change. We have some boundaries to tell us in which situation the solution will work and in which situation the solution may not work; i.e., one in which the basic conditions for effective change are, for some reason, impossible.

When and if the halcyon day arrives when the policy maker and officer holder will wait for the outcome of this entire process, the researcher will be able to say that his social solution has much scientific evidence and, as a matter of fact, is based largely on behavioral science. The following steps review the requisite phases of the research process.

1. *Conceptualization and Analysis:* The policy maker's problem is translated into several phenomenal models with differing observable consequences.

2. *Descriptive survey:* Indicators of the phenomenal models are constructed and used to gather data on a representative sample. The researcher reports the empirical generalizations concerning the differences between observed and expected outcomes and reports his judgments of which results constitute a violation of the ideal state of affairs. This report is returned to the policy maker so he can decide with which model he would like to proceed.

3. *Conceptualization:* After the client selects a phenomenon for further study, i.e., chooses one or more of the phenomenal models for explanation and potential manipulation, a theory is constructed to describe the process involved in the occurrence of the phenomenon. In other words, the researcher attempts to describe how some basic factors come to affect the incidence of the social problem.

4. *Explanatory research:* The researcher designs a series of tests, in a controlled analogue of the social problem, of the basic explanatory propositions involved in the theory. He has completed this phase when he has polished some explanations to the point where a highly controlled design will confirm his

thinking at several points in the process as well as in the predicted outcome.

5. *Engineering research:* The proposed manipulation is used in field experiments with many theoretically dictated checks on the process in operation and clinical checks for unanticipated deleterious consequences on people and organizations.

CURRENT DIFFICULTIES: THE SOCIAL SCIENTIST AND WASHINGTON

Race and education is a perfect example for analyzing the current relationship between the social scientist, the policy maker and an enormous social problem. The subject of race and education in America today presents one of the most tangled masses of values, facts, policies and research imaginable. Any professional commentator on the situation should quail before the size, complexity and state of ignorance. We know that there is a set of social facts presenting a terrible contradiction to the values of many Americans, policy makers and social scientists alike.

In some unknown way and from some essentially unknown reasons, the school, the chief source of upward social mobility in this country, is not functioning in a manner which allows children of poor black families to rise in the social structure, even to the point of being steadily employable with decent wages. Explanations for this failure range from failure due to family and cultural handicaps during the pre-school period, to the failure of the schools to meet the educational needs of these children, and finally, to the more lurid explanations concerning the basically racist nature of American society.

Answers Right Now.   The policy maker looks at the problem of race and education with an eye to "doing something about it." He typically works within a sharply defined deadline for recommended legislation. If he works with a social scientist directly, he defines the problem and demands immediate answers. The social scientist is in a quandary; he shares many values with the policy maker and would like to help if he possibly could. Yet, the first major block is the terrible time pressure. No amount of money can purchase the type of thinking, data collecting and thinking again that the best use of social science dictates. Should he then refuse to have any part of the task; or should he alter his scientific role and become part policy maker, using the data he can collect in a short time as a basis for some very educated guesses?

His decision can be dangerous as evidenced by the Moynihan contro-versy. Moynihan found himself *persona non grata* in many civil rights circles after attempting to advise the President on matters of social policy, using available census statistics to compute the correlations underlying his policy recommendations.[6] Even if the social scientist refrains from making policy recommendations directly and only agrees to do a survey, the pressure of time can short-circuit the conceptualization process and only allow for a partial analysis of the data as was the case with the Coleman Report.

Finding Favorable Evidence for a Policy. Sometimes the policy maker already knows what type of social solution he wants to see carried out; perhaps he would like to build a case for ending de facto segrega-tion of schools. He may build this case purely on political and value grounds; but when he decides that he would like to state that "better balanced racial composition will bring improvement in attitude and performance," we enter the realm of social science. This is an empirical proposition and may or may not hold under various conditions as yet unspecified. The trouble with calling in the social scientist to find evi-dence in favor of this policy is that a scientist is not like a lawyer preparing a brief for one side. The social scientist must formulate his problem independently and in such a manner that it is possible for him to be shown wrong. If he only collects evidence for one point of view, he has departed from his role as a scientist; and many social scientists simply refuse to be drawn into a working relationship with Washington on these terms.

Do facts speak for themselves? A third difficulty is much more subtle; the policy maker often believes that the role of the social scientist is to find the facts. These facts will speak for themselves, and facts have a certain solid reality in their minds. Before social scientists played such a direct part in government research, government collected statistics were used directly by the policy maker to check on potential social solutions. If the facts looked promising and the idea were a politically feasible one, expert witnesses might be asked to give an opinion on the recommended solution.

This self-styled social science tradition may explain the attitude toward the Coleman survey. It was a specifically commissioned set of data which could be used in much the same way as one would use census data. As we will show in the following chapter, the descriptive survey

---

[6] Lee Rainwater and William S. Yancey, *The Moynihan Report.*

by Coleman et. al., simply bursts with facts. Policy makers have examined principal findings and made recommendations for solutions on the basis of their own interpretations of the correlations. Coleman specifically warned against concluding causation from correlations, but the tradition of reading and interpreting the facts for oneself was far too strong to be swayed by any sociologist's warning.

From a professional analyst's point of view, the facts of the Coleman Report show that we don't understand why minority groups score lower on all tests than majority groups—no matter how persuasive the various explanations in current publications on educationally disadvantaged groups may sound. Methodologically, the Coleman Report raises extraordinarily complex issues concerning the author's attempt to tell which is the most important factor in the low performance rates of minority groups. Not only is there no sound basis for policy recommendations, but the mind boggles at constructing a reasonable, testable explanation for the observed results. Coleman and most other sociologists state that the answer lies in further study; but it will be difficult to convince Washington that the answer does not lie in combing through the collected data for the truth which they think lies buried under all the facts.

Uses of Correlational Data.   The policy maker usually feels he has shown much forbearance and respect for science if he waits to see the outcome of a descriptive survey before formulating policy. If the survey shows that minority group composition of a school predicts poor individual performance, he declares that science has shown that manipulating the school's racial composition will improve individual performance in minority groups. He disregards the social scientist's warning that this observed association is not necessarily evidence for a cause-effect relationship and that a single study taken at one point in time is insufficient evidence for a potential manipulation of racial composition over a period of time. "It's better than any evidence we've seen up till now; and the sample is both random and representative" will be the rejoinder to all the cautions and qualifications.

Here the difficulty between the scientist and the policy maker is a very simple one—the policy maker doesn't understand what correlations are and how they can be interpreted, *but he thinks he does.* The scientist must do studies in such a way that amateur interpretation is almost impossible. It is our position that the use of explicitly stated *abstract phenomenal* models as a reference for observations will help to reveal the technical nature of the research. The policy maker must not think that these correlations represent cause and effect in the real social world. These correlations were never intended to represent reality—they are abstractions with many implicit assumptions. But unless these abstractions and assumptions are spelled out it is not surprising that the layman believes that he is qualified to interpret and formulate policy on the basis of what he takes to be "facts" and "explanations."

"AFTER ALL, IT'S ONLY APPLIED RESEARCH."

Many social scientists are not particularly alarmed about the difficulties outlined above. They feel that we are making real progress when our studies are solicited by men of action. When compared to anything we have seen before, studies such as the Coleman Report constitute a great improvement in terms of sophistication and potential impact. If some of the haste in which the study was done is overcome by careful re-analysis of the data tapes, it is generally believed that we really are making progress in providing important bases for policy.

I am not so sure. I am very troubled about the human cost of making an erroneous attempt at solutions to social problems. If the basic researcher is wrong, nobody suffers for it but the investigator and his associates. If applied research, which is unsound, is taken seriously by men who have the power to act; or if perfectly sound applied research is interpreted incorrectly, there may be many school children who will suffer for the error. Policy claiming scientific validity in our times is policy with greatly increased chances of being enacted. Because of this, there should be no excuse for a lower set of standards for applied research. From an ethical point of view, nothing short of the best must be used for research on matters of social policy. If no time will be given for doing a proper job, then perhaps refusing to participate is the only power we have. If our work is read as if it were a magazine report then we must make clearer its technical nature. If pressures for certain types of legislation are too great, then we must perhaps retreat from the scene of governmental action to the university where we can discover any serious defects in the proposal. In summary, if we cannot say, in all good conscience, that a certain solution is based on the most powerful research we know how to do, then we must be content to let that particular proposal take its chances in the traditional political arena.

four

THE DIAGNOSTIC SURVEY OF
A SOCIAL PROBLEM

In the preceding chapter the first stage of the policy research process was briefly described as the construction of alternative phenomenal models in consultation with the clients (policy makers). We will now explore in more detail what the construction of these models entails, and the advantages of our method in comparison with more conventional approaches to descriptive surveys. Unfortunately, we cannot point to completed diagnostic surveys using this analysis method. We will use the Coleman Report where alternative definitions of equality of opportunity are employed in the gathering of data *but they are implicit rather than explicit*. By drawing out these implicit equal opportunity definitions and by clearly separating the concepts used for descriptive purposes from the same concepts used in explanatory data analyses, we will try to supply a thorough understanding of the use of phenomenal models in a diagnostic survey. The best current survey practice (as represented by the Coleman Report) is compared with an alternative method of survey conceptualization and analysis. The burden of proof falls upon us. The reader must be convinced that the advantages of a careful analysis prior to data collection outweigh the disadvantages of losing precious time.

First, we will explore the definition of "equality of opportunity" as "equality of facilities." We will try to show how explicit definitions of values could be developed through conferences with policy makers as well as explicit criterion statements, prepared before collecting data.

We shall then apply this hypothetical model to the data that Coleman collected because our criterion statements are based on the report's implicit assumptions. At each stage in the process of design, data collec-

35

tion and interpretation, we shall try to point out the implicit assumptions and abstractions which were involved in the Report and which could be made explicit. Something as concrete as "school facilities" cannot be measured until many abstract assumptions are made. These abstractions and assumptions, if made explicit, do affect the interpretation of the data.

The second part of the chapter explores the "educational outcome" definition of "equality of opportunity." A contrast is made between the model Coleman used and a hypothetical model with the following features: outcome operationalized in terms of occupational success and mobility; and economic factors held constant while examining racial differences in the benefits gained from education. The point of this comparison is to demonstrate the difference between the two models in usefulness for policy making and research. Future researchers may plan for maximum utility through a strategic formulation of the phenomenal model.

THE EQUAL FACILITIES MODEL

Clearly, one must start with what the policy makers want to know. Just what bothers them about the social scene? What values do they feel are being violated? In the case of the Coleman Report, Congress was concerned about the traditional role of the schools in providing equal opportunities for various groups in the society. The starting point for the Coleman Report is the following directive written into the Civil Rights Act of 1964:

Section 402, Civil Rights Act of 1964

The Commissioner shall conduct a survey and make a report to the President and the Congress, within two years of the enactment of this title, concerning lack of an availability of equal educational opportunities for individuals by reason of race, color, religion or national origin in public educational institutions at all levels in the United States, its territories and possessions, and the District of Columbia.[1]

The specification of particular groups in society, public schools, at each level and the exact geographical territories suggests that this directive is more concrete than it actually is. "Equality of opportunity in

---

[1] Coleman, *Equality of Opportunity*, p. iii.

education" means different things to different policy makers, depending upon their own value system.

ALTERNATIVE DEFINITIONS OF VALUE

In one traditionalist value position, all the members of a generation are in a contest for achievement and success; society should attempt to equalize accidents of birth by providing equal school facilities for everyone. Beyond that obligation, everything is left to individual drive and ambition. Peter Schrag aptly describes this value position in *Commentary*:

> Historically, "equality of educational opportunity" simply demanded that all individuals were to have access to similar resources in similar public schools: where children failed, it was because of their own limitations, their lack of ambition and intelligence, not because of the inadequacies of the schools or the society.[2]

Conferences with policy makers soon would reveal that some of them intended this definition of equality of opportunity. Other policy makers might want to examine evidence using this definition in addition to evidence using other interpretations of the value. The traditional definition of the value implies a particular phenomenal model very different from the more liberal definitions. The observables of the traditionalist phenomenal model would be school facilities, related resources, teachers, i.e., those features of the school environment generally felt to be conducive to education. Let us call it the Equal Facilities Model.

EXPLICIT EMPIRICAL CRITERIA

Having chosen a phenomenal level for study, we must consider some *explicit empirical criterion statements*. We need these statements before doing any data collection or analysis since the researcher and his clients must decide which events will force the conclusion that the results constitute an important departure from the ideal state of affairs and which results will be considered compatible with an ideal state of affairs. Following out our example of the Equal Facilities Model, at least two initial empirical criterion statements occur to the researcher:

(1) We will agree that the observed events constitute a departure from the ideal if we find significant variation in school facilities

---

[2] Peter Schrag, "Why Our Schools Have Failed," *Commentary*, 3 (March, 1968), 31.

between regions of the country, between urban and rural areas, or between social class and racial groups.

or

(2)   We will agree that the observed state constitutes a departure from the ideal state only if the observed variations in the quality of school facilities correlates with the race and social class group of the student.

These roughly stated alternatives would do as a starting point in conferring with the clients to discover which criterion statement will satisfy them as fulfilling the value. They may decide that they must live with a good deal of geographical variation in school facilities, considering the present method of school financing and the economic conditions in different parts of the country. They may decide that it is not variation *per se* that is troublesome but that it is the systematic variation discriminating in favor of the richer white population that conflicts with the idea of equal educational opportunity. These decisions would reveal that the initial attempts at criterion statements must be modified. The exact changing of these statements is the task of the researchers, but at the same time, the thought processes of the clients are undergoing clarification which will aid in the proper utilization of survey results.

The decisions of the policy makers suggest a very important qualification. Variations associated with geographical area will be expected, but, in and of themselves, they will not be regarded as violations of the ideal state. Rather, regions of the country will be used as controls in the presentation of the results.

We will have to analyze the term "systematic discrimination" a little further. The policy makers have pointed to an important difference between discrimination solely on the basis of race or social class as compared to discrimination on the basis of where you live (regardless of who you are). In other words, if Negroes live in poor rural Southern areas they may experience poor school facilities, but so will anyone else who happens to live in this area. To study discrimination on the basis of race, we must develop a criterion statement which holds constant a person's environment. If we want to include geography as a basis for discrimination, we will have to develop a second criterion statement in which we will consider the distribution of facilities for different racial groups within sub-areas (for example, the rural South).

In terms of feasible government action, the criterion statement making racial comparisons within areas is more practical. If we find facilities unequal for the races within a region, government subsidy might help to equalize the resources. If we find that the apparent racial inequalities are due to geographical variations in resources within a region, government action is also feasible. Without this statement using geographical controls, it is hard to see how the government could afford to do anything in response to a country-wide generalization on unequal facilities.

Notice that some criterion statements can produce results in a form readily usable by the policy maker. An important consideration in formulating these criterion statements is the awareness of a result which will allow the policy maker to make feasible suggestions. Of course, this is not the same as planning for the results you want to see; the empirical results may well show that the model is not violated. Statements of departure from the ideal state are not useful when they are so phrased that no conceivable federal policy or further research will improve the original state.

If the policy makers agree with this formulation of implications, we are now ready to make empirical criterion statements in a very specific form. They must be so specific that they constitute an *a priori* set of criteria for interpreting the survey's results. Only when these specific criteria are met, will the researcher decide that the observable constitutes an important departure from the ideal state.

If the Coleman Report had used the above method of analysis, two of their empirical criterion statements might have been formulated in advance of the data collection and would have looked like this:

(1) If Negroes are more likely to attend schools with *consistently poorer* facilities than whites who live in the same county and face the same regional school financing conditions, it is a departure from the ideal state of affairs.

and

(2) If Negroes and whites who live in the same county are experiencing consistently poorer school facilities than whites who live elsewhere within a given region and metropolitan or rural area, it is a departure from the ideal state of affairs.

Thinking ahead to the results based on these two criteria, there are at least two types of possible policy solutions. A possible finding of discrimination solely on the basis of race suggests a different intervention than does discrimination that comes from living in a poorly financed school district. Intervention under existing laws or new laws are potential policy solutions for evidence of racial discrimination. Plans for some form of federal financial aid to poorly financed school districts may be a policy solution if the departure from the ideal is only found for the second criterion statement.

How specific must the first empirical criterion be if we are seeking results amenable to a direct federal solution? First, we must state that we expect regional and urban-rural differences in the quality of school facilities and that these, *in and of themselves,* do not justify a statement of "unequal opportunities." Secondly, we must decide what we mean by a consistent result across different indices of school facilities. We can actually set up criteria in advance for judging a consistent pattern, such as evidence of discrimination on the basis of race across most of the indicators on a given dimension of school facilities. If desired, the size of the differences observed in the experience of whites and Negroes could also be taken into account.

What would the results of the survey look like? They would consist of empirical generalizations concerning the direction and consistency of the findings on the indicators. Following each dimension would be a judgment of whether or not the ideal model had been violated. We might see something similar to the following:

Empirical generalization: In the rural South, Negroes came out less favorably than whites who live in the same county on 9 out of 10 academic indicators of school facilities.

Judgement: According to our rules for judging consistency and according to our first empirical criterion statement, the observed constitutes a violation of the Equal Facilities Model.

COLEMAN REPORT—INTERPRETATION OF FACILITIES DATA

There are no hypotheses or predictions for the facilities' data in the final government report. Yet the authors did have some clear expectations for the direction of the results. Coleman stated what some of these expectations were in the *Southern Education Report* well before the publication of the findings.

. . . the study will show the difference in the quality of schools that the average Negro child and the average white child are exposed to. You know yourself that the difference is going to be striking. And even though everybody knows that there is a lot of difference between suburban and inner-city schools, once the statistics are there in black and white, they will have a lot more impact.[3]

---

[3] Jim Leeson, "Questions, Controversies and Opportunities," *Southern Education Report,* 1 No. 3 (November-December, 1965), 7.

Thus we see that a striking difference between Negro and white experience was predicted. Furthermore, the very design of the data tables and the sampling plan reveal similar expectations for a consistent pattern of black-white differences. The data tables were all designed the same way for each indicator of school facilities, giving the frequencies and the percentages by region, by degree of urbanism, by county and by race. There was no time for more than these analyses, so the authors were evidently gambling on these particular variables to slice the data into meaningful comparisons. If the results had been as predicted, there would have been an imposing array of tables all telling the same story of outstanding discrimination in school facilities in particular areas of the country for indicator after indicator.

But the results did not come out this way. When the authors attempted to interpret the resulting complexities, they ignored the original expectations which had never been formally incorporated into the report. Thus, they were not bound to state that the expectations were unfulfilled. Rather, they could puzzle over the empirical results and attempt to make the best *post hoc* interpretation possible.

Suppose that the implicit assumptions of the Coleman Report had been formalized as empirical criterion statements. What difference would it have made? They would have analyzed and measured the concept of school facilities differently. Obviously there would be sharp differences in the interpretation of what constituted a significant result. These differences in the design of indicators and rules for interpretations of the indicators would lead eventually to an interpretation *opposite* of the published version.

Sample Design. The very mode of sample selection in the Coleman Report reflected the desire to make comparisons between white and Negro school facilities in every area of the country. The investigators used a two-stage probability sample stratifying by region of the country and metropolitan-nonmetropolitan areas. The sample of nearly 600,000 public school students was specifically designed to select more heavily in minority group areas. The investigators were assured of plenty of children of each race to discuss in each locality of the country.

Tabular Presentation. In the introduction to the presentation of tables and in the arrangement of all the tables concerning school facilities, we see that the Coleman Report designed the comparisons to be the same as outlined in the empirical criterion statement. The tables all take the following form:

TABLE 1†

PERCENT OF WHITE AND NEGRO PUPILS ATTENDING SECONDARY SCHOOLS HAVING ART AND MUSIC TEACHERS, FOR METROPOLITAN AND NONMETROPOLITAN AREAS BY REGION, FALL 1965.

	United States			Nonmetropolitan								
				North and West			South			Southwest		
	N*	W(N)**	W***	N	W(N)	W	N	W(N)	W	N	W(N)	W
Art Teacher:												
No Art Teacher	33	32	29	52	48	42	79	81	70	59	54	68

	Metropolitan														
	Northeast			Midwest			South			Southwest			West		
	N	W(N)	W	N	W(N)	W	N	W(N)	W	N	W(N)	W	N	W(N)	W
Art Teacher:															
No Art Teacher	1	3	5	4	26	11	50	31	20	32	22	34	1	1	3

*N   = Negro
**W(N) = Whites living in the same counties as Negroes
***W   = White

†Adapted from Table 2.23.10, Coleman, *Equality of Educational Opportunity*, p. 89.

This arrangement of data allowed the investigators to compare Negroes and whites living in the same county while holding constant the region of the country, and the degree of urbanism. They also could compare whites who lived in the same county as Negroes with whites in the whole area. If whites in the same county as Negroes shared the Negroes' difficulties and both were, in turn, much worse off than whites in the area as a whole, the discrimination would appear to be on the basis of geography rather than race.

For many of the indicators, the use of region of the country and urban-metropolitan distinctions proved to be crucial control variables. Frequently, there were much greater differences on the basis of these control variables than there were on the basis of racial comparisons. The "absence of art teacher" shows this pattern quite clearly in the excerpt in Table 1.

OPERATIONAL DEFINITION OF SCHOOL FACILITIES

We have intentionally left this discussion until the end. What are the best indicators of a complex concept of this sort? There are three major dangers in selecting indicators for concepts in criterion statements. The first danger arises because the choice of indicators always implies an analysis of the concept's critical features. That original analysis may be wrong.

Analysis of school facilities' concept presents a perfect example of just how difficult the choice of indicators can be. Since we have no strong research or theory about which features of a school environment are critical for education, the researcher must return to those features generally believed by educators to be important. The Coleman Report becomes agnostic at this point, leaving to the reader the selection of those results on the indicators which he feels are the most important in the promotion of education. Any or all of these beliefs could be mistaken; and we could easily leave many critical factors out of consideration. Analysis of the facilities concept deals with which particular features of school facilities are important as well as with certain built-in ideas about the level on which they actually affect the student. For example, the Report did not deal with the interaction of the facilities characteristics with the special characteristics of the children. Some children may require more of whatever is measured, thus leaving less resources for others. This is particularly true in schools with many "problem" children who take up so much of the teacher's and specialist's time. An average amount of "x" per child may look very misleading in a district where there are many more children who demand and get the total supply of "x."

Secondly, there is the danger of selecting a poor indicator of a critical variable. Suppose we want to measure the quality of teachers, having agreed that their quality is a key feature of the quality of school facilities. Coleman selected such indicators as the years of training, the score on a test of verbal ability, the years spent in the school area, educational attainment of the teachers' parents, years of teaching experience, and whether or not they read professional journals.[4] These indicators comprise almost everything an ingenious investigator can place on a questionnaire. The quality of teachers may also be indicated by supervisor ratings or independent classroom observations. Observational indicators usually do not correlate well with teacher background variables. Many would argue that they are, however, far more closely related to how a teacher affects the student than an array of questionnaire variables. Results using observational indicators may look very different from results using questionnaire indicators.

Thirdly, an indicator may also suffer from insensitivity. For example, the only indicator of class size in the Coleman Report is the average pupil-to-teacher ratio over a whole school.[5] But, class size can and does vary widely within a given school, so our index does not give a very sensitive measure of the degree of classroom attention a student receives at the time of the survey.

To sum up these critical problems of the survey's choice of operational definitions, (1) we may have chosen the wrong or irrelevant features of school facilities for measurement in the absence of any useful research and theory concerning the effect of facilities on education, (2) the chosen variables may be operationalized incorrectly in that they lack any kind of construct validity, and (3) the measurements may not be sufficiently sensitive to capture important differences in educational environment. It now becomes obvious that the operationalization of the criterion statements is a highly technical task. Unfortunately the reader frequently does not realize that the results, in the form of data tables using different indicators, can be affected by all three of these problems. He never knows when to assume that a result is more accurate because it doesn't suffer from any of these ailments, or when to assume a result has become completely distorted by these problems. To reemphasize a most

---

[4] James S. Coleman, Ernest Q. Campbell, Carl J. Hobson, Alexander M. Mood, Frederic D. Weinfeld, and Robert L. York, *Equality of Educational Opportunity,* U.S. Department of Health, Education and Welfare, U.S. Office of Education (Washington, D.C.: Government Printing Office, 1966), pp. 122-48.

[5] *Ibid.,* p. 67.

important point: there is nothing concrete or real about results even though they measure something as tangible as a hot lunch program. They are based on a series of technical decisions and abstract analyses even if the authors do not consciously spell out the research process.

The implicit analysis of school facilities into a set of dimensions such as quality of teacher, academic resources, and other physical resources, each with a group of indicators, yields still another problem for interpretation. If these really are different dimensions of school facilities as they affect the education of the child, and if a group of indicators is chosen for each dimension, then the indicators of a single dimension should be more closely associated with each other than with those of other dimensions. If the indicators of a given dimension are closely associated, we can examine the results involving them with much more respect than the results involving indicators of a dimension which show no relationship to each other. In the Coleman Report, no material was offered on the interrelationship of the indicators, nor on the reasoning which led to the choice of the key dimensions of school facilities. We are forced to examine the thousands of results, one at a time—a formidable task for human understanding.

EXAMINING THE RESULTS

The percentages of Negroes and whites who have the advantage of certain types of school facilities within a given geographical area are sometimes the same, sometimes a little different, and sometimes very different in either possible direction. The percentages in the data table often fluctuate wildly; and the pattern of differences shows little consistency between the different indicators for elementary and secondary school. As was expected, very large differences were observed between regions of the country and between metropolitan and nonmetropolitan areas. Even these differences did not reveal a consistent pattern of thorough-going weakness in one particular area's facilities as compared to another area's. Rather, it was a patchwork pattern of lacks and availability.

Take for example, two indicators of an important dimension of school facilities—books. The survey queried the availability of free textbooks in different schools, and whether or not the textbooks were in sufficient supply. Let us examine the pattern of differences in percentages of Negroes as compared to whites living in the same county [W(N)] who had favorable experience in these two respects in two areas of the country, the South and the Southwest. In the diagram below we have symbolized the direction of the difference in the percentages by the symbols for "greater than" and "less than." The reader should note the results that are contradictory to the stereotype of Southern discrimination, and the inconsistent pattern between strata for a given region as well as the inconsistent pattern of two indicators' differences for a given area.

TABLE 2†

COMPARISON OF PERCENTAGES OF NEGROES AND WHITES WHO LIVE IN THE
SAME COUNTY AND WHO HAVE AVAILABLE FREE TEXTBOOKS AND A SUFFICIENT
NUMBER OF TEXTBOOKS: SOUTHERN AND SOUTHWESTERN REGIONS.

	South		*Southwest*	
	Met.	Non-Met.	Met.	Non-Met.
Free Textbooks	N > W(N)	N = W(N)	N < W(N)	N > W(N)
Sufficient Number of Textbooks	N > W(N)	N < W(N)	N > W(N)	N < W(N)

† Adapted from Table 2.21.14, Coleman, *Equality of Educational Opportunity*, p. 80.

What did the Coleman Report do to pull together this puzzle? There is a summary at the end of each section comparing the findings with racial differences favoring whites to the findings that differed from these. They attempt to speculate on how indicators showing the same general result can be combined to reveal dimensions of school facilities on a *post hoc* basis. The authors decided that the indicators more consistently showing racial differences favoring whites were more likely to be academic than indicators not showing these differences.

In stating these summary findings, inconsistencies within the tables were largely ignored. Although the authors carefully point out that regional differences are frequently greater than racial differences, the inconsistencies in the racial comparisons within the strata are really considerable. Again, using the sufficiency of textbooks as a rather straightforward academic indicator of the quality of school facilities, if we compare Negroes and whites in the same county and we count anything over a 2% difference favoring whites as an instance of discrimination, we find that Negroes are worse off in 4 of the 9 comparisons for secondary schools and 5 of the 9 comparisons for elementary schools. Can we really conclude that Negroes are less likely to have a sufficient supply of textbooks? The Report does state that Negroes are less likely to have textbooks in sufficient supply.[6]

---

[6] Coleman, *Equality of Educational Opportunity*, p. 122.

At this point we are considering in detail, how the Coleman Report handles specific results because the use of the phenomenal model would lead to a sharply different interpretation of the same findings. The Report's summary of the findings is falsely concrete leading superficial readers (and few have the time to check out the tables) to conclude that these statements are representative of "how things are."

Forgotten are the following points:

(1)   degree of consistency in pattern within a table
(2)   degree of consistency from indicator to indicator supposedly measuring the same dimension of school facility
(3)   lack of any information on the quality and power of any of the indicators used
(4)   lack of consideration of the size of the observed differences

In contrast, the diagnostic survey method here advocated, would make *a priori* decisions about the order of consistency from table to table which would be considered a violation or departure from the ideal state. Furthermore, we recommend knowing in advance something about what differences to expect between indicators supposedly measuring different dimensions, and indicators known to differ in sensitivity. We would specifically plan for expected regional differences by accepting as evidence of a regional departure from the Equal Facilities Model a pattern of Negroes with poorer school facilities than whites repeating itself throughout the rural South in all the analyses using indicators of a given dimension.

If Coleman had found such consistencies, he certainly would have reported them as important findings. The difficulties and differences of interpretation arise when things do not come out as predicted. The use of an Equal Facilities Model implies that the ideal state is *not violated* by the reported data. The Report's conclusions on school facilities attempt to capitalize on those scattered unfavorable racial differences that appear empirically, thus leaving the reader with the impression that the facilities favor the whites in important academic respects. But the two methods of analysis and interpretation of the *same data* leave the reader with opposing general conclusions.

EDUCATIONAL OUTCOMES MODEL

Although Congress wanted some data on the equal availability of school resources, there were policy makers who wanted a different phenomenal model of equality of opportunity. If you are very concerned about rapid upward mobility for some minority groups in this country, you will want to show what happens to these children as they proceed through the schools. Will they obtain the educational credentials necessary for decent jobs? This alternative phenomenal model, which we will call the Educational Outcomes Model, concerns educational outcomes as compared to inputs and was also implicit in the Coleman Report. The underlying reasoning is: if social inequalities in our society produce differential readiness to take advantage of the schools as they are now constituted then, *even if facilities were equal,* the disadvantaged child would not have an equal chance to succeed by the educational route. In order to have the "same" educational opportunity, this line of reasoning states, special compensatory features of the school should be in operation to allow a minority group to show the same variation in achievement as an initially advantaged group.

ALTERNATIVE DEFINITION OF "OUTCOME"

Few would argue with Coleman and his colleagues in their decision to examine inequalities in educational outcomes. However, people such as Peter Schrag,[7] would quarrel with studying academic achievement and ability scores as the only indicators of educational outcome. Schrag feels that equality of educational outcome should not be interpreted to mean that the average black should do as well in school as the average white or that resources should be poured into the schools until he does. Schrag does believe that such desired goals sound "pleasant" but impossible and "probably undesirable" if one assumes there are important cultural differences between ethnic and minority groups which have nothing to do with deprivation but rather with different socially valuable contributions.

At first glance, Schrag may look as if he belongs to the old, "We have great respect for the hewers of wood and drawers of water" school of thought. But he is not saying this at all. He is stating that, at the present time, schools deal with only a few of the valuable human competencies. Furthermore, ability and achievement tests are designed to measure a very limited range of these human competences in which the white middle class groups specialize. A change is needed in the philosophy of school curriculum, allowing the growth of a broad, diversified curriculum —a trading of the strengths various groups bring to the school—beyond the minimal educational requirements.

---

[7] Peter Schrag, "Why Our Schools Have Failed," *Commentary*, 3 (March, 1968).

If we follow this alternative definition of equal educational outcome we will examine phenomena different from the Coleman Report. With the Coleman Report interpretation of educational outcomes, it was perfectly logical to examine the achievement scores in different subjects at different grade levels for differing ethnic and racial groups. Taken to its logical extreme, Schrag comments that this interpretation of the ideal state will only be met empirically when Negro children from Harlem do as well in college board scores or reading achievement tests as whites from Scarsdale.

The implications of Schrag's definition of the Equal Educational Outcomes Model are complex and most instructive to follow. He would need some phenomena showing the educational effects of preschool deprivation as distinct from genuine cultural differences. He might examine the extent to which schools were overcoming these deprivations. Beyond this, he might examine phenomena such as eventual occupational outcomes through empirical criterion statements. These statements could concern undesirable differences in the degree of upward educational and occupational mobility among boys of different races who have disadvantaged fathers, and undesirable differences in the degree of downward educational and occupational mobility among sons of different races of more advantaged fathers.

The problem of selecting those students showing the effects of uncompensated deprivation as compared to effectively educated individuals not good at purely verbal tasks, requires a thorough search of the available research and theoretical literature on the educationally disadvantaged. So well accepted is the school's definition of intelligence that some concept of a bright child who takes what he needs from the school but is not a "success" in their terms would have to be carefully developed —it would be a striking new concept for most educators. Coleman's interpretation of educational outcome in terms of ability and achievement tests is more similar to the generally held beliefs of both laymen and school personnel. The empirical criterion statement in the Report's implied Educational Outcomes Model would deal with differences in the distribution of achievement scores between minority groups and the white majority. The results indicating a violation of equality of educational outcomes would be judged on *a priori* criteria of the degree of difference between these distributions of test scores.

COLEMAN'S MODEL

Given the definition of equal educational outcomes and its measurement in the Coleman Report, the results showed a flagrant violation of ideal conditions. With dogged consistency, the Negro group scored below the dominant group or any other ethnic group. Although the scores also differ by region of the country, the pattern of ranking scores, in terms of ethnic groups, repeats itself at different grade levels and in different regions of the country.[8]

Minority pupils' scores are as much as one standard deviation below the majority pupils' scores in the first grade; this difference is accentuated by twelfth grade. The overlap of distributions is not as large as might have been predicted: 84% of the children in the minority group are below the median of the majority students. Regional variation in achievement scores is much greater for Negroes than for whites at each grade level. Whereas the difference between majority and minority increases between first and twelfth grade in the metropolitan South and Southwest, there is no such increasing disadvantage in the metropolitan Northeast. This tells the investigator only that some very complex environmental factors work on the individual with differential time effects. The Negro appears to be more sensitive to these environmental effects than the white.

In the next chapter, we will study the problem of attempting to explain the survey's major results. At this point, we can all agree with the authors that the outcomes represented a flagrant violation of their version of the ideal. We can also see that this particular outcome suggests no particular policy. In order to conceive of any policy, we must understand why we are observing these major differences in test scores. This is in contrast to certain outcomes we might have seen on the Equal Facilities Model which would have given policy makers legal grounds for intervention when they saw the empirical results indicating systematic discrimination. It is not surprising that the authors, when presenting the descriptive results, hasten to attempt an explanation of the variation in test scores by various types of background factors.

The solely descriptive phase of the study could have been more useful; the results could have more clearly implied the nature of the search for explanation. Just why the results were so puzzling will be thoroughly discussed in the next chapter. Even though the report uses the somewhat more commonsense definition of educational outcomes, Schrag's interpretation could have led to more practical results.

SCHRAG'S MODEL

Suppose, that at this point, we trace the implications of Schrag's definitions of equal educational outcome, employing empirical criterion

---

[8] Coleman, *Equality of Educational Opportunity,* 218-74.

statements before data collection. The criterion statements would consider the frequency of deprivation effects in different racial groups as opposed to the mixture of deprivation and a cultural preference for non-verbal tasks. Descriptions might deal with the educational status of children from very poor, overcrowded homes. The success of these children in overcoming their handicaps would be examined among the different minority groups and the white majority group in different areas of the country. We would expect children from economically disadvantaged homes to show less academic success, on the whole, than children from richer homes, regardless of minority group membership.

The policy maker must know if we are failing universally to compensate for pre-school handicaps; or if we are failing selectively with certain minority groups. In our attempt to explain possible racial variation in the early stages of academic success, we might refer to our facilities data on compensatory programs in the schools of poor children of different races. If we find no program difference correlated with success or failure, we might examine the idea that some specific treatment and structural and power shifts in new ghetto schools are necessary for some minority groups.

Professional commentators on the Report wonder why Coleman *et al.*, did not examine differences in achievement scores for minority and majority groups, controlling social class. If our theory of the Report's implicit definition of educational outcomes is correct, then it was not necessary to use social class in the description. The authors wanted to examine departures from an ideal state where the effects of both race *and* social class were nil.

To summarize this discussion of equal educational outcomes, we are in perfect agreement with the Coleman Report that, given its implicit assumptions about how equality of educational outcome should appear on a phenomenal level, its data do constitute a flagrant violation of the ideal state. Yet, we feel that alternative definitions of equal educational outcome, such as Schrag's, would have led to results with more heuristic value. The Coleman Report's results leave us confused as to where to look next for explanation. The alternative phenomenal model discussed above, would tell us precisely where to proceed in our search for explanatory factors.

ADVANTAGES OF BEING EXPLICIT

The method of survey conceptualization here described would be time consuming when pressures for immediate answers are now enormous. Why should a social scientist wait for the time to have a series of detailed conferences with the potential users of the survey? These conferences would deal with the type of information the users wanted. Our basic argument is that, if the results of the survey are incorrectly interpreted, or even worse, misinterpreted by the policy makers, then the investment of time and money in the survey was not worthwhile. Furthermore, if the results of the survey are in a form not useful for direct policy suggestions or not useful for deeper explanatory research, then the survey was not properly designed for its intended purposes.

To review these difficult points, we cannot leave the interpreter on his own to decide which data he finds sufficiently alarming because he may not realize that any survey conclusions of "severity" and "extensity" are relative to the definition of whatever value is under investigation. To illustrate: because of the implicit definition of equal educational outcomes Coleman uses, his decision was not to control social class, causing the differences in achievement scores to look positively horrifying. The educated layman does not realize that some score differences are attributable to socioeconomic differences, while some are attributable to racial differences. If the socioeconomic differences were controlled, the "severity" of the results would be somewhat different. In the proposed method, it becomes very apparent that results refer only to an abstract technical model. The reader will discover that the Equal Facilities Model leads to a finding of no violation of the model while the Equal Outcomes Model leads to a finding of departure from the ideal state in all parts of the country. The layman will (1) realize these are technical, abstract matters and (2) realize that he cannot quote broad statements about the findings without some of the assumptions on which those findings were based.

Secondly, the non-scientific reader tends to substitute his implicit idea of the value for the implicit idea used in the research, because it was never sufficiently explicated. Suppose the reader defines educational outcomes in terms of the knowledge acquired as a result of his schooling which is functional in the individual's life and uses Coleman's test score descriptions as an index of this working knowledge. He may be quite mistaken. Such an implicit model dealing with functional learning might use very different kinds of behavioral observations for its phenomenal level. Unless carefully cautioned, he may read entirely too much meaning into a comparison of test scores.

In a different vein, we have argued that the self-conscious use of phenomenal models can lead to information outcomes that are more useful in decision making. A sophisticated awareness of this linkage, can lead the researcher to choose deliberately a set of criterion statements

which will yield information relevant to a course of conceivably successful social action.

The user, too, should be aware of the link between the type of social
action implied by the results and the model. He may then reject the
implied social action because he rejects the assumptions in the model in
the first place. This is the key to the argument for explicit model-build-
ing. A social scientist engaged in applied research such as a survey of
equal educational opportunities knows the step beyond description is
discussion of a course of action. His report of the resulting generalizations should clearly take this fact into account.

The readers and users of the survey must be made to understand that
not only the type of social action but also the type of *causal variable*
examined depends on the initial definition of the value's phenomenal
meaning. If under the Equal Facilities Model we are dealing with
systematic discrimination against Negroes in school facilities within a
given rural, regional area, we will closely examine the power variables in
that area. If we are dealing with the Educational Outcomes Model, we
will examine variables such as the climate of depressed area schools
which might account for low performances. The possible social action
to remedy a situation will, therefore, look very differently in these two
cases. The first might be a political or legal solution to increase the
minority group's power to demand resources. The second type of social
action might involve investment in special educational innovations to
manipulate school climate and therefore raise performance levels.

The researcher must indicate to both the reader and user of his results
what kinds of inferences concerning social action can and cannot be
made safely from the results. The use of one model may indicate direct
social action. For example, if one designed a model to examine departure
from strictly constitutional procedures granting equality in schools, the
results could imply direct legal intervention. Results from something
similar to the Educational Outcome Model, indicate no direct social
action can be safely inferred. First, one must decide how these achievement differences come about; and then one must experiment with altering
the process favorably. Descriptive or correlational results of the initial
survey will not be sufficiently powerful for the policy-makers to decide
what kind of social action is desirable.

In review, if our definition is the narrow one of school facilities and
suggests investment as a remedy, and if we find that minority groups are
receiving fewer of any of those facilities considered valuable, we will not
be too worried if the policy maker decides to invest in better standardiza-
tion of school facilities. Even if the socioeconomic factors better explain

the finding than the racial factor, there is little harm to be done. In contrast, as soon as the model includes educational outcomes measured by achievement scores, and the minority groups show a consistently low level of achievement, the policy-maker should not infer whatever he pleases. It is incumbent upon the researcher to analyze and investigate the complex of causes that result in differential achievement. This is a mammoth conceptual and empirical job which no descriptive survey possibly can complete; this can be foretold from the first formulation of the model. The user of the survey should know exactly what the results will imply for the length of the research program before social action can be safely recommended.

five
ACHIEVING MORE POWERFUL
EXPLANATIONS

Presently, federal policy makers cannot or do not utilize the more powerful methods of social science explanation for policy statements about manipulating social variables for social betterment. Whether this occurs because of the social pragmatism of a government style which prefers a trial and error approach accompanied by the constant bustle of "doing something," or whether it occurs because of the failure of the social scientists to demand time for better explanations, is not at all clear. Nevertheless, if the social scientist can provide the policy makers with a dramatic empirical demonstration of the extensity and severity of a social problem, and with suggestions of some underlying factors through a correlational technique, the policy makers are content with this information for the generation of politically feasible proposals for social action.

The social scientist must then content himself with the role of a catalyst who promotes a sufficient sense of urgency to merit the investment of money into social problems. Because he is aware of certain problems, the social scientist is not sure that these policies will be reasonably effective and will do no harm. He is well aware of the following problems:

1. Policy statements are often cause-effect propositions where certain resources are manipulated to bring change in social situations.

2. The preliminary correlational analyses of a correlational survey are not a satisfactory basis for the construction of cause-effect propositions.

3. Social phenomena appear to be caused by such a complex of interacting factors that there is actually a very high probability of

one of these policies being quite wrong, because the underlying notions of cause and effect are weak.

4. Not only will a wrongly conceived policy fail to bring about desirable improvement in the social problem, but it may well bring about unanticipated deleterious side-effects.

The researcher, realizing the uncertain degree of confidence one can place in the "explanations" offered in a simple sample survey, attempts to warn the reader not to place too much confidence in the significant association of one variable with another. For example, the authors of the Coleman Report repeatedly caution the reader that these correlations are not positive proof of cause-effect relations.

But do people really believe that, "correlation does not prove causation?" When Coleman and his interpreters attempted to move from correlational results to policy implications, this caution about correlation appeared to have been thrown to the winds. In a rather dizzying way, authors of interpretive articles state the need for caution when dealing with correlation and then propose policy *assuming* that the predictive factors are explanatory factors. Authors further assume that if these explanatory factors were manipulated in ways dependent upon their creative fancy, there would be an improvement in the achievement scores of minority groups.

Merely mentioning the need for caution is not sufficient. These interpreters of the data fail to use their imaginations in an equally fertile fashion to imagine how wrong, as well as brilliantly right, they may be. We are given only a set of policies that sound reasonable in the light of current popular discussion; we have no way to assess the possibility of the policy being quite wrong or the consequences of a wrong judgment.

SOURCES OF ACHIEVEMENT
A MULTIPLE REGRESSION ANALYSIS

In this chapter we would like to examine Coleman's most elaborate correlational analysis of the potential sources of achievement among minority groups. Without going into the technical statistical questions this correlational analysis has raised (which have been covered elsewhere in the available literature), we would like to discuss the problems of transition from correlational analysis to policy implications. We must look briefly at the logic of the multiple regression technique used by the Coleman Report, the kinds of interpretations that were made in the body of that Report, and the kinds of policy implication drawn from its analysis elsewhere in the journals. By examining the problem of alternative explanatory factors and alternative modes of measurement, we hope to convince the reader of the possibilities of any interpretation of this type of an analysis being wrong as well as being right. Finally, drawing from the above analysis, certain suggestions will be made for the initial design of a survey, remembering this critical problem of developing explanations suitable for policy purposes and leading to data capable of less tenuous interpretation.

THE PREDICTION OF ACHIEVEMENT SCORES

The distributions of scores for some minority groups on an ability test in the Coleman Report were distinctly below the distribution of scores for the majority group. This finding by itself does not imply policy. It does demand some explanation. Assuming that we are very unhappy with the test score differences observed, we will not be able to prevent such differences until we understand how they came about.

When the investigators originally planned for the investment in comparison of test scores, they must have realized that if the scores differed for the minority groups (and all previous studies indicated that they would), there would have to be a search for explanatory factors. Other than including data on a tremendous number of variables connected with schools and individuals, there seems to have been no particular planning for the testing of explanatory hypotheses. As in so much of today's survey research, an elaborate correlational technique—the multiple regression analysis—was used to bring forth the factors which were the most probable potential causes of the phenomenon. For this purpose a number of single questionnaire items which have a conceivable causal effect on performance were grouped under the general headings of school characteristics, individual background characteristics, student body characteristics, and student attitudes. The authors knew that great care would have to be exercised in estimating the strength of any one of these general groupings since they tend to be interrelated. In other words, it is known that children from poor families tend to go to poorly financed schools, filled with other poor children, all of whom tend to share attitudes not conducive to good scores on achievement or ability tests.

The multiple regression analysis, in simple terms, is a statistical technique controlling one set of variables while the association between another predictor variable and the dependent variable is examined. In the analysis of test scores, individual background variables were entered first. They estimated the portion of variance in test scores these variables could account for. Then, school characteristics, a second set of variables, were entered into the analysis; estimates were made of what *additional portion* of the variance in test scores could be accounted for by these school factors. The additional portion of the variance was small in comparison to the portion of the variance accounted for by the initial entry of individual background variables.

In the summary of this analysis the authors carefully cited the "relatively small amount of school-to-school variation in test scores that is not accounted for by differences in family background"; they refer to "the small, *independent* effect of variations in school facilities, curriculum, and staff on achievement."[1] Furthermore, the Report specifically warned the reader of the interpretation of this analysis:

> There are a variety of precautions necessary in interpreting the results of such analyses. They do not prove that the factor caused the variation; they merely indicate that the two are related. For example, if we found that per pupil expenditure accounted for much of the variation in achievement, the relation might nevertheless be a result of factors which are themselves associated with both achievement and expenditure, such as the economic level of the families from which these children come. In many cases these factors can be statistically controlled, but cautions in interpretation remain necessary.[2]

The Report itself avoids drawing policy implications from its correlational analysis.[3] Instead, it makes careful statements avoiding the as-

---

[1] James S. Coleman, Ernest Q. Campbell, Carl J. Hobson, Alexander M. Mood, Frederic D. Weinfeld, and Robert L. York, *Equality of Educational Opportunity*, U.S. Department of Health, Education and Welfare, U.S. Office of Education (Washington, D.C.: Government Printing Office, 1966), p. 325.

[2] *Ibid.*, p. 292.

[3] The Report's use of the multiple regression technique has come under sharp attack. Levin and Bowles give an excellent discussion of its problems in their article, "The Determinants of Scholastic Achievement—An Appraisal of Some Recent Evidence," *Journal of Human Resources,* III (Winter, 1968), 3-24. Coleman has answered this criticism in "Equality of Educational Opportunity: Reply to Bowles and Levin," *Journal of Human Resources,* III (Spring 1968), 237-46; the controversy continues into the summer issue. In reviewing Coleman's technique of first "controlling" for student background before examining the role of school resources, a task force at Harvard headed by Mosteller concludes, "the things used to control were so highly correlated with the things being adjusted that school effects were largely removed. . . . In problems where we have such strong correlation between background characteristics and where the situation is utterly confused, the adjustment can be misleading." (Henry Levin, "What Differences Do Schools Make?" *Saturday Review,* (Jan. 20, 1968), p. 66. See also Glen Cain and Harold Watts, "Problems in Making Inferences from the Coleman Report," Discussion Paper, Institute for Research on Poverty, (University of Wisconsin, 1968). These authors criticize the lack of theoretical framework to provide order and rationale for the inclusion of variables in the analysis. They also criticize the criterion used to assess the statistical performance of the variable as inappropriate for policy-making purposes.

sumption that the analysis has told us anything of what could or could not be accomplished through further investment in school facilities. They also avoid the implication that they have produced evidence of the *total effect* of past investment in school facilities. Statements of the effect of school facilities are conditional. They refer to predictive power, only if one remembers the prior entry of individual background factors as predictors.

REPORTING ON THE "REPORT"

In discussing the Report's results, educational, scientific and literary journals quickly forgot the limitations of this statistical analysis in estimating the total power of school facilities to produce changes in performance. Although the pertinent section from the Report's results is quoted verbatim, the commentary by various authors suggests that they either do not fully understand this statement or for lack of any better information, they assume that they are dealing with a pretty fair estimate of the total power of school facilities and background characteristics to produce achievement.

Take, for example, Jim Leeson's commentary in *Southern Education Report*. He carefully quotes the following section of the Report:

> The relatively small amount of school to school variation that is not accounted for by differences in family background, indicates the small *independent effect* [italics mine] of variations in school facilities, curriculum and staff upon achievement.[4]

Leeson then summarizes this result as an "explosion of an assumption" about American education, i.e., "School quality has less effect on achievement than the student's family background and the social environment of the student body."[5] He has lost the important qualifying word, "independent," and we see the beginning blurring of correlation and causation.

Coleman himself in an early commentary on the Report, ventures to suggest policy implications of the survey. Given his results, he suggests the following as one of the avenues to equal educational opportunity:

> For those children whose family and neighborhood are educationally disadvantaged, it is important to replace the family environment as much as possible with an educational environment—by

---

[4] James Leeson, "Some Basic Beliefs Challenged," *Southern Education Report*, II, No. 9 (1967), 3-6.
[5] *Ibid.*

starting school at an earlier age, and by having a school which begins very early in the day and ends very late.[6]

Although he makes other major suggestions, two key points can be made with this suggestion. Note that we have specifically suggested manipulations dealing with a *time span* of the child's experience. Coleman proposes that the child begin school earlier in order to produce improvement over time. But remember, Coleman draws from results dealing with students *at one point in time*. Any inferences involving change over a period of time drawn from these results are, by definition, tenuous.

Secondly, note that his suggestion assumes that a correlation between family background and school performance is due to the quantity of exposure to the family rather than quality of exposure to the family or quality of exposure to the school. It also assumes that schooling of an unspecified variety will alter the effect of the family—although an often quoted result of the Report is that the longer the children are in school, the greater appears to be the disparity between minority and majority group scores. To make a suggestion for policy like the one above, one has to imagine some process occurring between the predictor variable and the predicted. But remember that the survey did not formulate these ideas about process in a way that could be tested in the analysis of the results. There is no test in the survey of the quality of any ideas concerning how the predictor variable becomes associated with the predicted. If the policy suggestion involves assumptions concerning the nature of the causal processes and these processes are unexamined, the suggestion could be an incorrect one.

How thoroughly does the policy-maker, reading Coleman's suggestions, understand these untested and hidden assumptions? Does he realize that the study itself offers no assurance of the effectiveness of this particular manipulation as opposed to some other? And does he realize that the suggestion is based on untested ideas of how performance is lowered by family factors? Or encouraged by school factors?

Another example of an interpretation of the Coleman Report involving tenuous "inferences for policy" may be found in Dael Wolfle's editorial in *Science*. Wolfle interpreted the Coleman Report as presenting massive support for the generalization that differences in school achievement are so interrelated with differences in family background that changing school facilities and curricula would have little effect in overcoming deep-seated environmental handicaps. He concludes that schools only slightly influence a child's achievement independently of his back-

---

[6] James Coleman, "Equal Schools or Equal Students," *Public Interest,* I, No. 4 (Summer, 1966), 74.

ground and general social context. He further concludes that the inequalities imposed on children by their home, neighborhood and peer
environments become inequalities with which they confront adult life.[7]
A gloomy picture! His conclusion provides the impetus for those who
do not wish to spend more money on public education!

In a letter to the editor of *Science* on June 16, 1967, John Gilbert of
the Harvard Computing Center, Frederick Mosteller of Harvard's
Statistics Department and twenty-three others cogently criticized this
kind of careless interpretation and expressed deep concern lest this interpretation have an undue effect on policy. They firmly pointed out, as
we did in the previous example, that this survey is not evidence of the
effects of *changes* in investment in school facilities because of the inherent time interval limitations in any simple cross-sectional survey.
Secondly, they reject the inference that "children might as well stay at
home because changes in facilities probably won't do any good and
aren't doing any good now." They further stress that the small "independent" effect of school characteristics may be because the school
characteristics are almost inextricable from background characteristics,
i.e., poor schools tend to be in poor neighborhoods. The letter proceeds
to speak specifically to the problems of policy formation:

> . . . we run the risk that suggested hypotheses will be considered
> proven principles. Because of this danger we feel that great caution
> must be exercised in basing policies upon this part of the
> Coleman report [regression analysis]. The Office of Education,
> Coleman and the academic community must have more time to
> investigate the many facets of these data, not only by careful
> examination of the study itself but also by carrying out some of the
> many *experiments* [italics mine] suggested by the results in the
> report.[8]

A final example is important because it attempts to use the weight of the
survey's results to decide an important current policy controversy. Jencks,
after reporting the survey's results in *The New Republic*, combines his
interpretation that there is "a good deal of indirect evidence that this
kind of innovation (pouring more money into Negro schools) has made
very little difference in the past," with his conviction that Negroes will
do better if they are shifted to integrated settings.[9] These two interpretations imply a policy of investing our moneys in plans for racial balance

---

[7] Dael Wolfle, "Editorial," *Science,* CLVI (April 7, 1967), 19.

[8] John Gilbert, Frederick Mosteller, "Educational Data Open Questions,"
Science, CLVI (June 16, 1967), 1435.

[9] Christopher Jencks, "Education: The Racial Gap," *The New Republic,* CL
(Oct. 1, 1966), 25.

within schools rather than in educational innovations for predominantly Negro schools.

At the risk of being repetitious, let us state once more, that there is no evidence in the survey, direct or indirect on the process of innovation. Furthermore, no specific measure of compensatory programs was used in the regression analysis. This kind of conclusion, even though labelled "tentative," throws unwarranted weight behind one side of the current controversy over investing in racially balanced schools vs. doing something different than we have been doing with Negro schools. The design of the Coleman Report is inappropriate for answering this question.

DANGERS OF DRAWING POLICY IMPLICATIONS

Lest the reader think our criticism of the published implications of the regression analysis in the Coleman Report is much too severe considering the urgency of these serious problems, let us list the various ways that interpretations based on such an analysis might be quite wrong.

UNTESTED ASSUMPTIONS ABOUT PROCESS

Policy statements usually involve the recommended manipulation of a cause-effect process. We often attempt to suggest a policy from a correlation which merely examines the question: How powerful is this variable as a predictor of a social phenomenon? We are then forced to invent ideas about the causal process, ideas untested in the correlational analysis. Obviously, if we are wrong in our ideas about process, the policy statement will be a poor one. Any type of correlational analysis, completely lacking in tested process ideas of *how* the predictor variable comes to be associated with the dependent variable is a relatively weak form of explanation.

UNTESTED ASSUMPTIONS ABOUT TIME

Policy statements usually involve suggested changes that will, in time, bring improvements. To test these ideas, one needs a study with a "before" and an "after" measurement. This is usually an experiment which tests the association between a given manipulation and improvement in the same population over a period of time. If limited to a survey examination of people who have experienced innovation, we must make tenuous assumptions about what these people were like prior to social intervention.

AN ALTERNATIVE THEORY OF CAUSATION

As in any correlational analysis, there is always the possibility that some unmentioned factor is a more important condition than any variable used in the analysis. In other words, the predictor may not cause the observed association, but the action of an entirely different variable might account for co-variation.

In an excellent letter to *The New Republic*, Floyd McKissick suggests such an alternative hypothesis to Jencks' reasoning that the failure of facilities investment to produce improvement in Negro achievement implies the need to move in the direction of integrated schools for improved achievement. McKissick speculates that the investment of money in school facilities for Negroes has failed, *not because any investment* fails, but because there are other factors at work in these all-Negro schools which amount to a comprehensive system of "designed retardation." Among these other factors, he discusses eloquently the possibility of the parents' powerlessness to influence the type of education their children are receiving, and the inability the children feel to control their own environment. To reinforce this point he cites one of the Report's correlations: "A Negro child's achievement is very highly correlated with his feeling that he can control his own destiny."[10]

We have no more evidence that McKissick's hypothesis is correct than we have evidence that Jencks' hypothesis is correct. If McKissick is correct, and something in connection with power is the variable we should manipulate to improve performance, *we would be entirely wrong to take* children even further from the control of their parents by placing them in the alien environment of the white school. There is nothing in the results of the Report's correlational analysis that is inconsistent with McKissick's hypothesis. If power were the important variable, and if power is more closely related to the socioeconomic and racial status of the parents than to school facilities, then it wouldn't be surprising to find a weak association between facilities and performance and a strong association between individual and student body characteristics and performance.

The introduction of another explanatory variable is so important that we would like to propose still another explanation for the observed results. The Coleman Report deals with school-to-school variance and with factors accounting for portions of this variance. But suppose that a factor within the school is very important in producing poor performance.

---

[10] Floyd McKissick, "Is Integration Necessary?" *The New Republic*, CLV, No. 23 (Dec. 3, 1966), 33-36.

Suppose that the way in which teachers relate to low status children, especially black low status children, is a key factor in low performance rates. As John Neimeyer states, "The chief cause of low achievement of the children from alienated groups is the fact that too many teachers and principals honestly believe that these children are educable only to an extremely limited extent."[11] This alternative explanation confuses the clear-cut lines of the Report's regression analysis between school characteristics (which include teacher variables) and student characteristics. It suggests an important interaction between teacher and type of pupil. It further suggests the process of a self-fulfilling prophecy: a teacher's expectations for the low status student are based on social background; the student somehow senses this expectation and turns in a low performance to match the low expectation of success.

This hypothesis is an alternative way of accounting for the low scores of minority groups. As in the case of the power hypothesis, the results of the regression analysis are not inconsistent with its possible operation within schools.

No satisfactory secondary analysis of the data already collected could test the power hypothesis or the "expectations" hypothesis. The proper variables are not included in the study. Furthermore, the most appropriate test for either of these hypotheses is an experimental rather than a "post hoc" correlational study.

FINDINGS DEPENDENT ON CHOICE OF INDICATORS

In the correlational analysis we have been examining, a different choice of indicators for concepts such as individual or family characteristics might yield a different pattern of correlational findings. A different pattern of correlational findings obviously will yield a different policy implication. No rationale is given in the Report for the particular choice of indicators of school facilities, family background or student body composition. Levin and Bowles suggest that if the income and occupation of the Negro student's parents had been used instead of education, individual background factors would have been a more powerful predictor of test scores and student body quality would have been weaker as a predictor.[12] The possible choices of different indicators are infinite,

---

[11] John Neimeyer, "Some Guidelines to Desirable Elementary School Reorganization," *Programs for the Culturally Disadvantaged* (Washington, D.C.: Government Printing Office, 1963), p. 81.

[12] Henry M. Levin, Samuel Bowles, "The Determinants of Scholastic Achievement—An Appraisal of Some Recent Evidence," *Journal of Human Resources*, III, No. 2 (Winter, 1968), 3-24.

which means that estimates of the relative strength of a set of highly intercorrelated predictor variables are dependent on the nature of the indices selected.

The particular indicators of student body characteristics in the Coleman Report are an odd assortment from various levels of abstraction. For grades 9–12 they are: attendance, amount of homework reported, number of student transfers, proportion whose families own encyclopedias, and proportion planning to attend college. Where is the rationale connecting these variables? Although the investigators do not add the scores on these indicators but aggregate the power of each predictor to account for variance in the test scores, the conceptual problem remains the same. In what sense may we aggregate concepts of such a great intellectual assortment and call them, *in toto,* student body characteristics? Student body characteristics comprise a set of an infinite number of potential variables.

We need some idea that enables us to decide which student body characteristics are relevant to achievement. With some ideas of how student body characteristics affect achievement, we will know more about which facets of student body quality we want in our measurement. If the researcher postpones a theoretical justification for his choice of indicators until after the data are in and then tries by empirical techniques to uncover "underlying factors," he must worry that if he had measured his factors differently, his findings would have looked quite differently.

ASSIGNING MEANING TO MEASUREMENTS

In the Coleman Report the difference in test scores between minority and majority groups is considered the survey's major finding, but the concept that the "ability" test is supposed to measure is not clear. Thus, we may assign meaning to the results incorrectly, or we may be unable to assign any meaning to the results.

We know that these test scores will predict marks in school and therefore entry into college. But we know nothing about the various kinds of human learning that they do not cover. There are many intellectual skills necessary to success in the workaday world that are not reflected in this chain of predictions. We need to study, for policy purposes, learning which gives greater flexibility in moving through the occupational structure. It is not at all obvious that we are using a suitable test.

Coleman, *et. al.,* attempt to tell us what these tests measure. They are largely a measure of the amount of the dominant culture each person has gathered. The danger of inference from an "ability" test with the middle class biases toward inherent ability is thus avoided. But if the test measures the amount of dominant culture gathered why should Negroes have lower scores than American Indians or Mexican-Americans? From an anthropological and geographical point of view, both of these ethnic groups are more isolated from dominant American culture than the American Negro.

Thus, we are not confident that the tests measure what they are supposed to measure. We are forced to consider the results a gigantic riddle and attempt to deduce just what the test scores probably reflect. We must come to some conclusion or we cannot assign meaning to the results.

Regional variation in the scores of this test and in the scores of achievement tests at each grade level is greater for Negroes than for whites. Whereas the difference between majority and minority groups increases between first and twelfth grade in the metropolitan South and Southwest, there is no such increasing disadvantage in the metropolitan Northeast. This finding can only tell the professional interpreter that some very complex environmental factors are associated with the scores, and that these complex factors interact with the passage of time. Environmental fluctuations are more common among blacks than whites.

If we want to measure the benefits of schooling we would ideally find a measure free of the peculiar things that happen to people when they take tests. Often, people confuse test-taking with learning and too quickly assume that a test is a perfect measure of what one knows. This is a peculiarly dangerous assumption to make in the case of Negroes. There is growing evidence that specific test-taking disabilities in the black population may contribute to falsely low scores. In the chapter on interracial interaction disability, we will discuss this literature which suggests that disabilities operate where there is an implicit comparison with white peoples' scores or where there are white testers. Such a test-taking disability might explain why even Negro teachers do not score as well as white teachers on the survey's test of verbal competence.

In review, we are not sure we have for the Negro group a measure of the type of learning functional for upward occupational mobility. We also cannot interpret differences in scores on this test because we cannot make adjustments for specific test-taking disabilities probably operating differentially in the various minority groups. Furthermore, we do not know how the cultural biases in a test predicting grades affect the scores of different minority groups. The observed differences in test scores are extremely difficult to interpret because we have not carefully attempted to design interlacing measures of a theoretical concept of some type of learning. Rather, we have used the criteria that school personnel currently use to judge the probable success in conventional contemporary school curricula.

LIMITATIONS OF THE QUESTIONNAIRE

If we assign meaning to findings based on a questionnaire including unreliable items, large non-response problems, and without evidence of construct validity, we may make uncertain inferences. The questionnaire in the Coleman Report attempted to measure attitudes toward school. The results were reported in terms of the analysis of a single item purporting to measure an underlying attitude. It is hopeless to assign meaning to the results of any single attitude question. The difficulty of using questionnaire techniques with low status Negroes is one of many factors making the response to any attitude question doubtful. Unless we determine that the responses relate sensibly to each other and to outside criteria, the answers are meaningless.

We can see the problematic features of the Negro pupils' responses to the questionnaire used in the Coleman Report through the following list of oddities:

1. When comparisons are made for the U.S. as a whole, Negroes are the least likely of any ethnic group to attend a school with a high college attendance rate, have the lowest probability of enrolling in a college prep course and have the lowest probability of an over-all high school grade average of A or B, but they are only 1% less likely than the whites to plan on attending college in 1966-67 and 9% more likely than the whites to say "they probably will go to college in 1966-67."[13]

2. They have the highest probability of any ethnic group of reporting that the teacher expects them to be one of the best in their class.[14]

3. They have the highest probability of wanting to be one of the best in their class.

4. They have the highest probability of reporting that they never play hooky.

5. At the secondary level, the Negro students in every region are more likely than white students to report that their parent wants them to be one of the best students in the class.[15]

---

[13] Coleman, *Equality of Educational Opportunity*, p. 193ff.
[14] *Ibid.*, p. 193.
[15] *Ibid.*, p. 187ff.

6. The Negro student is more likely to report parents' attendance at PTA meetings than the average white.[16]

7. Despite the generally held belief, Negroes do not report being read to less often when they were pre-schoolers.[17]

8. On attitudes items for 12th grade students, the non-response rates for the Negro groups are unusually high; they often range between 20 and 25%, which is higher than the non-response rates for Indian-American or Mexican-Americans.

The large non-response rates present a critical problem for interpretation. In conventional pre-testing, such a large non-response rate is an important signal to the investigator to omit or to change the question, or even better, to interview the respondent. Does he understand the question? Does the question arouse hostility, anxiety, defensiveness so that the subject simply avoids answering? This may have been the case for many Northern metropolitan 12th grade blacks. If a large non-response rate persists in the final data, the data analyst must decide how to treat the non-respondents. In the Coleman Report, it was assumed that the non-respondents were identical to the respondents. If hostility and defensiveness produced non-response, the assumption of similarity is incorrect because their real answers might change the final results.

The simplest interpretation of the unlikely results gathered above is that the blacks are not using the same frame of reference as whites to answer the questionnaire. Many of the results are, in light of already completed studies, not believable. The answers are suspiciously school-oriented, normative, and perhaps designed to give the "white man" or "schoolteacher" the answer that he wants. It also prevents the possible anxiety and danger coming from revealing anything of real importance to the outsiders.

This may sound like paranoic behavior, if true. But sympathetic observers of black school children feel it is quite possible. When the white man's frame of reference is used (as it obviously is when a standardized questionnaire is being administered), all kinds of defenses may come into play. Open hostility may appear in the form of refusing to answer; and covert defensiveness may appear in the form of normative answers —what "Whitey" wants to hear.

Pfautz, in his symposium review, published in the *American Sociological Review*, shares this author's skepticism of the questionnaire's results:

[16, 17] *Ibid.*, p. 187ff.

There is little or no explicit appreciation of the possibility that ego-involved survey questions might produce "normative" answers. This may be a considerable factor in the finding that Negro teachers report reading more professional educational journals than white majority teachers, or in the replies of minority group students that their parents are highly interested in their education. Indeed, the tenuous linkages that often inform the analysis,—from the pupil reports of parental characteristics, to parental characteristics, to abstract conceptualizations of "orientation" to the school systems as a means of social mobility—suggest the sometimes uninhibited enthusiasm of the researchers. More restraint is called for when using the shot-gun face-sheet approach to data collection, an approach that often produces differences so small as to be inconsequential or in directions that defy cogent interpretation and suggest sheer factitiousness.[18]

As a matter of fact, the questionnaire may be an ineffective way of studying the Negro student—an alarming thought! There is no doubt that the questionnaire is a misused and overly used technique. Questions often are asked in areas that respondents cannot or will not answer frankly. We often have ignored the effect a highly verbal technique, used by high-status investigators, may have on low status rather non-verbal respondents. Studies of low-status blacks in the educational setting should consider the alternative techniques of behavioral observation and unobtrusive measures.

THE INITIAL SURVEY:
PAVING THE WAY FOR EXPLANATIONS

How can the investigator within the limits of an initial survey restricted to correlational analysis, avoid all these problems of interpretation? How can he build explanations with less tenuous implications for policy? Again we are struggling with the problem of planning for results in which meaning can be assigned with more certainty. For purposes of assigning meaning to a description, the last chapter suggested the use of a phenomenal model as a point of reference for the emerging empirical generalizations. In this chapter we suggest that the investigators plan to collect data in the initial survey designed to put some alternative explanatory ideas to a correlational test.

---

[18] Harold Pfautz, William Sewell, Leonard Marascuilo, "Review Symposium," *American Sociological Review*, XXXII, No. 3 (1967), 482.

Assume that plans for descriptive data involve the examination of achievement differences between minority and majority groups. If there are large differences in achievement scores the investigator should be prepared to test some explanatory ideas. Suppose that he has a rough idea such as, a very poor Negro in one of our larger cities has a sense of being powerless to control his school experience which leads to a progressive "tuning out" of school influences and a poor school performance with a high probability of drop-out. Here he is merely sketching the outlines of a very complex social process. If he wants the best possible test for these ideas within the limits of correlational data, he will conceptualize items like "powerlessness," "tuning out," "poor school performance," and "probability of drop-out." In a series of pre-tests, he constructs reliable measures with some evidence for the construct validity of these concepts.[19]

It is possible to construct some arguments about the way in which these variables should relate to each other if the results are consistent with ideas about the process. The most difficult problem is the status of the "powerlessness" concept. This variable may predict academic performance, but "powerlessness" could be a *reflection* or a *result* of poor work and drop-out rather than a potential cause. The multivariate technique can explore these possibilities in correlational data. If he controls academic performance and only studies individuals who are doing poorly, will the "powerlessness" variable predict "tuning out" and drop-out from school? If it is an antecedent of poor performance rather than a consequent variable, it should continue to do so. In contrast, if he controls feelings of powerlessness, and only studies individuals who feel relatively powerful, the ability of poor academic performance to predict "tuning out" and dropping out should be greatly reduced. According to his ideas he should also find that feeling powerless predicts "tuning out" behavior more strongly for economically and ethnically disadvantaged pupils than for other kinds of pupils. In turn, "tuning out" behavior should strongly predict low school performance and a high probability of dropout among disadvantaged groups who feel powerless.

---

[19] If you are clearly restricted to questionnaire techniques in the initial survey, then the possibility of normative responses should be checked by tabulating questionnaire responses with other kinds of information about the individual. When measuring attitudes, proper pre-testing can sift out items with large non-responses and select items which relate to each other in a manner indicating that the respondent at least is operating consistently across items. Here the researcher interested in such questionnaire techniques should undertake study of the various question scaling techniques available (Likert, Guttman, etc.).

He cannot regard these results as strong proof for his ideas, but he will have shown that *these data are not inconsistent* with his ideas.

Note that the analysis is narrowed to a choice of potential patterns of explanation rather than an attempt to maximize prediction. Even if the researcher were to collect a set of variables accounting for all the variance in performance, he still might have no knowledge of a process which can be consciously manipulated to improve performance. If he reasons that there are different subgroups in the larger minority group who fail to learn because of the operation of different processes, the antecedent condition for any one of these processes will not appear an important predictive factor in a multiple regression analysis. The assumption that prediction and explanation are the same is very dangerous if the most useful form of explanation is conditional and complex.

The fit of the correlational data to the pattern of ideas constitutes the criterion of the explanation's potential usefulness. Confidence in the style of explanation will develop if various measures of the same concept and measures of different concepts relate to each other and to the dependent variable as anticipated. If they fail to relate as predicted, some other measure of the concept may be tried on new data, or the measure may remain the same while the pattern of explanation is altered. At least there is some criterion for intellectual progress.

If the data fit the pattern of explanatory ideas, it is still necessary, in order to be intellectually honest, to detail the possible inaccuracies in the assumption that the correlational evidence presents a picture of a cause-effect process. As explained above, alternative explanations can always be entertained in correlational analysis. The use of statistical controls in the correlational analysis may eliminate some of these alternative explanations. Most likely, it will be necessary to plan a new research design specifically to eliminate alternative explanations.

After this, the researcher is prepared to begin the experimental phase of the research process. He has learned something about a possible explanation. (Very likely he has explored several explanatory hypotheses in the initial survey.) He knows a good deal about measuring the key concepts in these hypotheses and their attendant propositions. He has estimated the necessity for a reconceptualization or dropping a particular hypothesis as not particularly heuristic.

His next task may be to observe a ghetto neighborhood where parents have become more powerful. He might compare this observation with a similar ghetto neighborhood where parents are not powerful in the school. If he can find neighborhoods where the status factors look alike but the major difference involves successful activism in the school, he could compare attitudes of the children and his measures of motivation and performance.

If the observation agrees with his hypothesis, he may try a manipulated situation, where the experimenter helps the parents to become more powerful in the school and observes the results in an experimental and control group. There are various sociological theories available which could suggest concepts and propositions useful in characterizing this process of change.

This method involves something of a gamble. When only a few explanations are chosen for exploration, and time and resources are devoted to formulating concepts and designing measures of these concepts, there may be a negative result with the correlational patterns not fitting the hypothesis. The survey report may appear unimpressive in comparison to 400 tabular presentations based upon 400 different questionnaire items.

But again, it is our contention that even negative results will be less possible to misuse and can be more meaningfully interpreted than the more conventional alternative, 400 tables and all. The data have been designed to test a few chains of reasoning, not many possible chains of reasoning. The technique of correlation determines if the data are consistent with policy alternatives. It does not "discover" relatively powerful predictors. The reader should realize that policy solutions are dependent on the whole explanatory chain and not just the correlation between the first link and the end product. A discussion of the quality of the measurement makes clear the possibilities of misinterpretation arising from this source. The formulation of key concepts prevents the reader from substituting his idea of "school characteristics" for the concept underlying the survey's measurement. The reader can realize what concept he has tried to measure, and how adequate that measure is. Above all, the policy maker, hopefully, is ready to wait for additional evidence before concluding that he knows anything at all about the manipulation of a social problem.

six

EFFECTS OF RACIAL COMPOSITION: A CONTROLLED COMPARISON SURVEY*

What happens when survey results become relevant to a hotly debated political controversy? Evidence from completed surveys is dragged into one or the other side of the argument; whichever sounds more convincing may prevail. In a recent court case, the judge even found on the basis of "factual," i.e., correlational evidence, that the practice of tracking in high school had harmful effects on students (Hobson vs. Hansen, 269 F. Supp. 401, 1967), and ordered the schools of Washington, D.C. to end tracking according to ability tests.

The current controversy over integration of schools vs. quality education (or compensatory education) in racially imbalanced schools is a good example of using correlational data to bolster either argument. Tremendously complex value and political issues underlie this controversy; and nothing is particularly rational about the terms in which it is being argued. If the history of the controversy had not made the sides so rigid, it might even be possible to see integration as one form of compensatory education. The social scientist does not have to play any part in the settlement of the controversy; it could be settled in terms of politics and the values of the relevant pressure groups. But when advocates of integration argue that evidence such as the Coleman Report "proves" integration is the only solution to educational problems, the social scientist becomes professionally much concerned. His reputation hangs, so to speak, on one side of a complex controversy, yet his original study was not specifically designed to answer such a question.

---

* Co-authored with Bernard P. Cohen, Professor of Sociology, Stanford, California.

Even if he can gather data on the question, the terms of the controversy are not of his own choosing. Ordinarily, it is better to have a wide choice of questions for study as then the researcher may choose a question with an identifiable phenomenon for scientific study, a question with theory available to conceptualize a process between hypothesized cause and effect. On an abstract level, what kind of a phenomenon is school integration? Furthermore, how would a proposed change in the racial composition of a school affect the performance and attitude of the children? We are uncertain as to identification of the phenomenon for study; we have no ready made ideas for characterizing the process by which institutional structural features affect individual attitudes and behavior. The documentation of "structural effects" is of comparatively recent interest to sociologists. They have not yet constructed any tested explanations.

Furthermore, the controversy implies many empirical propositions stated as universals, for example, integration will benefit all minority group members equally; and integration in any form will produce benefits rather than damage. The scientist examines the problem conditionally. He doubts that any survey of his would support these propositions in universal form. He would prefer to phrase the question as "What are the conditions under which the alteration of racial composition will produce decreased prejudice in whites or increased learning in blacks?" Past work in educational research suggests that what will benefit one type of student may be detrimental to another. The scientist knows in advance that he needs some freedom to analyze the problem for study and that he must prepare the clients for results with "qualifying" tags.

Just how does school composition affect the child? Lacking any ready made hypotheses about critical features of school composition, perhaps the best method is to gather evidence in a controlled field experiment. Schools with similar clientele and curriculum could be divided into a desegregation treatment and a control treatment. Children experiencing desegregation could be compared to children of comparable background in comparable but segregated schools. Unfortunately, practical considerations do not permit such a study because in the areas considering integration, the lines of community conflict are so complex and have so hardened that no one will permit a rigorous experimental approach.

To gather evidence on the controversy at all, the scientist is forced to use a correlational approach with its previously discussed problems. In conventional practice, this means that he collects a random sample, including data on many variables; these data are subject to a *post hoc* analysis in which the achievement of minority groups in segregated and desegregated situations is compared. Certain variables, such as social class, are held constant in the analysis because they may also account for any observed relationship between integration and better school performance. These survey data are used for both descriptive and explanatory purposes; descriptively they estimate characteristics of the population from the characteristics of the random sample; they also examine the relationship between hypothesized cause and effect such as the association between integration of schools and performance.

The major difficulty in using data collected for descriptive purposes in a *post hoc* correlational analysis is that the study is not designed in terms of a thorough analysis of the problem. All the other difficulties actually follow from this lack of a relationship between the design of the study and the analysis of the problem. For example, one cannot usually make the key comparisons in a *post hoc* analysis with sufficiently stringent controls. Unless one plans ahead of time to measure certain factors which serve as control variables, the best indices available are not usually included in the already collected data. Unless the sample is extremely large, one is very likely to run out of cases in critical comparisons. Again, *unless one plans ahead of time* for the kinds of comparisons that are important, there are not usually enough cases with the right characteristics falling into a random sample. These two difficulties are closely related, because one is *especially likely* to run out of cases when an index with a complex character is used for control purposes.

In this chapter we would like to suggest, by means of a detailed analysis of the integration problem, use of the literature, and the development of an actual research design, an alternative approach to the gathering of data on a concretely phrased current controversy. Our recommended approach should be of general usefulness in cases with the following characteristics:

1. Evidence is desired to settle an empirical question concerning the educational effects of a proposed manipulation.

2. The terms of the controversy are not in a form easily identifiable as a scientific phenomenon.

3. There is no readily available theory for the construction of hypotheses to explain the relationship between manipulation and effect.

4. A rigorously controlled field experimental approach is out of the question.

In these cases, the social scientist may turn to a strategic survey with design features different from those in a conventional sample survey. We call this design a "controlled comparison survey." Because this design only clarifies the relationship between variables under different conditions, estimating characteristics for the population as a whole is not compatible with the design and cannot be handled by it.

CONTROLLED COMPARISON SURVEY

In essence, the controlled comparison survey consists of selecting examples from nature for observing the way in which two variables relate to each other *under differing conditions*. The social class of blacks may relate in one way to performance in integrated schools and in another way in segregated schools. Examples from nature are carefully selected to allow comparisons between cells that differ in one condition but match in other important conditions. The generation of data, illustrating the relationship between the antecedent and consequent variables under different social conditions, hopefully will stimulate theorizing concerning the process by which these variables appear to relate to each other. In most cases, the scientist can make prior predictions of the degree of association between the variables for different conditions.

This operation requires a thorough analysis of the conditions under which the relationship is expected to vary. Intellectually, it is not very different from deciding the important control variables in a *post hoc* analysis, except that the choice of control variables in the controlled comparison survey, is made before and determines the nature of a survey design. For example, if the researcher thinks that the social class of the black child differentially affects his reaction to integration vs. segregation, the researcher can plan to find an example of a group of middle class black students who have experienced segregation as opposed to a group of middle class blacks who have experienced integration. Because he has not collected his data, he has the opportunity and the obligation to make a thorough analysis of what the concept of "middle class" means to a Negro population. This early analysis allows him to decide upon a careful index for selecting "middle class black" cases. Not only does a controlled comparison survey necessitate a careful analysis of the important conditions likely to produce variation in the relationship of the key variables, but also a careful analysis of the nature of the independent and dependent variables. What is a "segregated situation"? Does it depend upon the percentage of the population that are minority group members or does it depend upon parents and students defining the school as segregated? Does integration improve performance, attitude, or lower the probability of dropout? If considered in advance of data collection, these questions can lead to plans for indices of several different concepts relating to the antecedent variables and the consequent variables.

DISENTANGLING SOCIAL CLASS AND RACE

The educational effect of racial composition is an excellent method of illustrating this survey design because it exhibits a classic problem of control. When we want to estimate the effects of racial composition, we find ourselves inextricably tangled with the question of social class. Separating the effects of racial composition from those of social class composition is not a simple matter. A high proportion of all black schools are also schools with a lower social-class composition; there is a strong correlation between being black and being of a lower social class in the public schools. Because of this correlation, one may attribute to racial segregation those harmful educational consequences that may be due to class composition or to segregation by social class. This may, in part, be true; but there still may be special effects of *de facto* segregation beyond those of the slum school. How can one examine the question: What is the special effect of being an all-black school beyond the effect of being homogeneously lower class?

Many of the proposals for promoting racial balance in the public schools fail to distinguish between the undesirable effects of an all-black school and those effects due to the general problem of the slum school, be it all-white, all-black or racially balanced. The failure to distinguish between social class factors and racial composition factors may lead to inadequate practical recommendations for the improvement of Negro education. It is hardly surprising that the practitioner does not make this distinction as most contemporary social research restricts itself to the study of either racial or social class composition.

The problem of control variables is complicated further by the necessity to control social class both at the level of collective properties (school composition) and at the level of individual properties (social background of the individual). Most of the available studies have focused on the attributes of the individual students. To understand the effects of altering the racial composition of the schools, we have to understand the relationship between properties of the collective and properties of the individual; we must somehow separate the consequences of racial factors from those of social class factors.

To illustrate the interaction between properties of the individual and properties of the school, let us consider a young black of low socioeconomic status. Will he perform better if he attends a racially balanced school rather than an all-black school? Past research predicts that it depends upon other features of the school. If the racially balanced school is also predominantly middle class, while the all-black school is homogeneously lower class, the performance differential is likely to be greater than if both schools are homogeneously lower class. The same question could be asked about a young black from a middle class background. Notice that in our example we have varied (1) an individual property—the social class of the youth and (2) two collective properties —the racial and social class composition of the school. This question indicates the important conditions of variation we will want to build into the survey design.

FORMULATION OF THE PROBLEM

The problem is fundamentally one of "contextual analysis."[1] That is, we want to describe an individual in terms of his own attributes and in terms of properties of his social context. In this formulation the school attended constitutes a social context or collective; racial composition is a *property of the collective*, not a property of the individual.[2] Previous research on race and the schools concentrated on collective properties or individual properties, but rarely both types of properties. A typical study at the collective level is a comparison of the average performance of students in a predominantly white school with the average performance of students in a predominantly black school. The most common approach has been the examination of individual properties, as exemplified in studies comparing school performance of white and black students without regard to the schools these students attend.

   Not only is it necessary to study the individual and collective levels simultaneously, but also there must be *two individual properties* and *two collective properties*. The formulation of the problem is complex; but the necessity for a contextual analysis utilizing four variables comes from a conviction that anything less leaves the practitioner doubting the relative importance of racial composition of the school in the educational problems of black youth.

---

[1] Paul Lazarsfeld, "Evidence and Inference in Social Research," *Daedalus,* LXXXVII, No. 2 (1958), 99-130.

[2] A collective property is really a property shared by all members of the collective. Thus, attendance at a predominantly black school is a property of every student attending that school.

ONE COLLECTIVE AND ONE INDIVIDUAL PROPERTY

To illustrate our formulation and the inadequacies of simpler formulations, let us examine, in graphic form, what the previous designs can tell us. Table 3 represents a collective property, the racial composition of the school and an individual property, race of the individual. In this table the x_{11} refers to an average measure of one of our dependent variables—performance, aspiration or attitude. For example, x_{11} might be the average achievement for whites attending a predominately white school; x_1 would be the average achievement score for all whites in the study.

TABLE 3

THE EFFECTS OF SCHOOL RACIAL COMPOSITION
ON INDIVIDUALS OF DIFFERING RACE

School Composition

Race of Individual	Predominantly White	Predominantly Black	"average"
White	x_{11}	x_{12}	$x_{.1}$
Black	x_{21}	x_{22}	$x_{.2}$
"average"	$x_{1.}$	$x_{2.}$	

The typical studies mentioned, only deal with average qualities of *either* collectives or individuals. In this illustration, a comparison of $x_{1.}$ and $x_{2.}$ would be a comparison of performance in predominantly white schools and performance in predominantly black schools, without regard for the race of the individual. These studies immediately lead to the question: Are these performance differences a function of the schools' racial composition or a function of the race of the individuals involved in the comparison? Similarly, any simple comparison of the average performance of whites and Negroes ($x_{.1}$ vs. $x_{.2}$) leads to the question: Is this difference a function of the type of school or the race of the individual?

Some studies have compared x_{11} and x_{22}, whites in predominantly white schools and blacks in predominantly black schools. Such a comparison is poor because the race of the individual and the composition of the school are different. A true contextual analysis would avoid this difficulty by involving all four cells of Table 3 which would enable us to attribute priority to one of the two types of variables.

With the contextual analysis one may find a crucial interaction effect beyond the main effects of the row and column variables on the dependent variable. That is, being a Negro in a predominantly white school may turn out to be different from being a Negro in a segregated school. If our study designed on the basis of Table 3 found that blacks attending predominantly white schools showed better performance than blacks attending segregated schools, a fresh question would arise: Aren't these students attending predominantly white schools more likely to be middle class and therefore have higher performance and aspiration levels, regardless of the kind of school they attend? Regardless of the race of the individual, the social class factor may account for performance differences. We know that social class is related to our dependent variables by previous research documenting the performance and aspiration differential of middle class and working class students.

TWO INDIVIDUAL PROPERTIES AND ONE COLLECTIVE PROPERTY

The quality of contextual analysis depends upon the selection of important row and column variables, i.e. the choice of individual and collective properties. Optimally one should select variables, each with a demonstrable relationship to the dependent variables of the study. To avoid being left with the troublesome social class question one must consider the social class of the individual in the research design. Table 4 represents the joint consideration of two individual properties (race and social class) and one collective property, racial composition of the school.

TABLE 4

THE EFFECTS OF SCHOOL RACIAL COMPOSITION ON INDIVIDUALS OF DIFFERING RACE AND SOCIAL CLASS

School Composition

Race of Individual	Social Class of Individual	Predominantly White	Predominantly Black
White	Middle Class	x_{11}	x_{12}
	Lower Class	x_{21}	x_{22}
Black	Middle Class	x_{31}	x_{32}
	Lower Class	x_{41}	x_{42}

The paradigm in Table 4 allows a number of different comparisons. One interesting comparison is the differential effects of the school's racial composition on middle vs. lower class Negroes. If we found that attendance at a predominantly black school were associated with a low level of performance for middle class Negroes, we still would have the question: Is the important characteristic of the predominantly black school its racial composition; or is its lower social class composition the key to low performance? Since predominantly white schools are more likely to have a middle class composition than predominantly black schools, how do we know that class composition is not more important than racial composition for variations in all comparisons involving different school types?

TWO INDIVIDUAL AND TWO COLLECTIVE PROPERTIES

Several studies have shown the importance of a school's social class composition in accounting for variation in aspiration and performance. When the social class composition of the school is included, we arrive at the paradigm for the present study as shown in Table 5.

TABLE 5

THE EFFECTS OF SCHOOL RACIAL AND SOCIAL CLASS COMPOSITION
ON INDIVIDUALS OF DIFFERING RACE AND SOCIAL CLASS

		School Composition			
		Middle Class		Lower Class	
Race of Individual	Social Class of Individual	Predominantly White	Predominantly Black	Predominantly White	Predominantly Black
White	Middle Class	x_{11}	x_{12}	x_{13}	x_{14}
	Lower Class	x_{21}	x_{22}	x_{23}	x_{24}
Black	Middle Class	x_{31}	x_{32}	x_{33}	x_{34}
	Lower Class	x_{41}	x_{42}	x_{43}	x_{44}

In principle, the study design shown in Table 5 would allow us to make the crucial comparisons. These comparisons would enable us to assign relative priorities to class and racial factors. Unfortunately, however, some theoretical types may not exist empirically. For example, at the present time, it is highly unlikely that one would find enough predominantly black schools that are also predominantly middle class. Therefore, we immediately strike the second column on Table 5. Another problem cell may be x_{14} as there may not be enough middle class whites attending predominantly black lower class schools. Even though we are unable to represent every cell, the paradigm indicates many useful comparisons.

Suppose the practitioner is examining data on the performance of lower class Negroes in three different school settings: predominantly white middle class (x_{41}); predominantly white lower class (x_{43}); and predominantly black lower class (x_{44}). If the difference between the predominantly white lower class school and the predominantly black lower class school were greater than the difference between the two predominantly white schools of different social classes (x_{43}-x_{44} vs. x_{41}-x_{42}), he could infer that lower class Negroes should be moved into white schools, regardless of the social class composition of that school. Recommendations different for middle class Negroes than for lower class Negroes may well arise from examining x_{31-4} of the design.

RELATED RESEARCH

In our formulation of the problem, we noted that the choice of independent variables should depend upon previously observed relationships to our dependent variables. In this section we shall review previous findings concerning these relationships. First, however, we shall indicate our basis for choosing these particular dependent variables.

We accept the importance of performance as a dependent variable because it is the obvious measure of the school's effectiveness in raising the status of the Negro. Because of our interest in the prospects for black upward mobility, we next choose some measure of occupational and educational aspiration. Most of the present relevant research uses these two variables of performance and aspiration.

However, besides providing channels for upward mobility, the school has other potential functions for the black student which are often confused with the mobility function. Among these other potential functions are: (1) to create black youth who will be employable in a society where the minimal required skill level is rapidly rising and (2) to reduce the possible significant alienation of black youth from our society. In spite of these variables' obvious importance, there is little systematic research directly concerning them. A school setting which is most effective in raising aspiration and performance levels may not be the most effective in reducing the proportion of alienated individuals. Therefore we must include attitudinal measures to avoid a completely one-sided picture of the consequences of school composition.

Turning first to aspiration, researchers repeatedly have found the strong relationship between a student's social class background and his level of aspiration which remains strong even when IQ is carefully controlled.[3]

---

[3] For a review of these studies, see William H. Sewell, Archie O. Haller, and Murray A. Straus, "Social Status and Educational and Occupational Aspiration," *American Sociological Review,* XXII, No. 1 (1957), 67-73.

The studies of race and aspiration, unlike those of social class and aspiration, are far too contradictory. A great effort has been made to distinguish between occupational aspiration and occupational plans. The plans are supposed to have a greater reality element than aspirations. Stephenson finds no differences between Negro and white aspirations, but the plans of white students are higher than the plans of Negro students.[4] If the comparison of racial groups is made for a given social class, Wilson finds *no differences* in the aspirations and plans between Negroes and whites.[5] In contrast, two studies (Sprey, and Holloway and Berreman) find that Negroes have *significantly lower* aspirations and plans than whites.[6] Finally, Gist and Bennet[7] examine the relationship between race and aspiration for separate social class and IQ groupings and find no racial differences in aspirations or plans.[8]

What can be safely concluded about the relationship of race and aspiration? First, it is necessary to control the social class factor because of its well demonstrated relationship to aspiration. Secondly, once social class is controlled, the relationship is not clear and is probably dependent upon a number of not well-understood conditions. We can infer some of these conditions from Rosen's study of achievement, motivation, and cultural values involving achievement in mothers and sons of various ethnic and racial groups.[9] Although Negroes were lowest on the motivational measure, they were not the lowest in valuing the striving ethic. If this part of the black value system is similar to the over all American orientation, and if aspirations are more related to values than to motivational drives, then we would expect black and white aspirations to be similar. In any case, it can be hypothesized that class is more important than race in determining occupational aspiration.

Beyond the social class of the individual as an important predictor of aspiration, there is evidence of the effect on aspiration of the collective

---

[4] R. M. Stephenson, "Mobility Orientation and Stratification of 1,000 Ninth Graders," *American Sociological Review*, XXII, No. 2 (1957), 204-12.

[5] Alan B. Wilson, "Residential Segregation of Social Classes and Aspirations of High School Boys," *American Sociological Review*, XXIV, No. 6 (1959), 836-45.

[6] Jetse Sprey, "Sex Differences in Occupational Choice Patterns Among Negro Adolescents," *Social Forces*, XLI, No. 1 (1962), 11-23. Robert G. Holloway and Joel V. Berreman, "The Educational and Occupational Aspirations and Plans of Negro and White Male Elementary School Students," *Pacific Sociological Review*, II, No. 4 (1959), 56-60.

[7] Noel P. Gist and William S. Bennet, "Aspiration of Negro and White Students," *Social Forces*, XLII, No. 1 (1963), 42.

[8] These studies used different questions to measure aspirations and plans, different indices of socio-economic status, handled "don't know" categories very differently, and used subjects of different ages.

[9] Bernard Rosen, "Race, Ethnic and Achievement Syndrome," *American Sociological Review*, XXIV, No. 1 (1959), 47-60.

property of the social class composition of the school attended. Using the individual's social class and the class composition of his school in a contextual analysis, both Wilson and Michael find a strong association, for a boy of a given status background between the school attended and plans to attend college.[10] These studies suggest that beyond the effects of family background, are effects on the individual's educational plans which are related to the social class of high school peers. A working class boy who goes to a middle class high school is more likely to plan on college than a working class boy attending a working class high school. Conversely, a middle class boy attending a working class high school is less likely to plan on college than a middle class boy attending a middle class high school.[11]

When we consider performance as a dependent variable, we find more research involving the racial composition of the school attended. Simple comparisons of performance in predominantly black and predominantly white schools such as we described in Table 3 are available. Comparisons in Gary, Indiana, and Plainfield, New Jersey, show a significant gap in performance between Negro and white schools, with the Negro schools showing the poorer performance.[12] Even when the collective property of the school's social class is added to the analysis, Deutsch finds that performance in a Negro school is poorer than performance in white schools of similarly low socioeconomic status.[13] Data from New Rochelle suggests that (1) if the comparison is made between black students only and (2) if the schools are located outside a homogeneous slum area, the school's racial composition does not seem to be related to performance. Negro performance in Lincoln school, the *de facto* segregated storm center of the New Rochelle litigation, is not inferior to the performance of Negroes in less segregated schools.[14] In contrast, Wilson notes that the school's social class composition for an individual of a given social class is *positively related to performance.*[15]

---

[10] Alan Wilson, *op. cit.* John A. Michael, "High School Climates and Plans for Entering College," *Public Opinion Quarterly,* XXV, No. 1 (1961), 585-95.

[11] In a study currently being analyzed by Wallin, of a group of schools with some socioeconomic range but all outside a big city, the relationship between social class composition of the school and educational plans of the boys failed to appear.

[12] Max Wolff, "Segregation in the Schools of Gary, Indiana," *Journal of Educational Sociology,* XXXVI, No. 6 (1963), 251-61.

[13] Martin Deutsch, "Minority Group and Class Status as Related to Social and Personality Factors in Scholastic Achievement," *Society for Applied Anthropology Monographs,* No. 2 (1960).

[14] John Kaplan, "New Rochelle: A Report to the U.S. Commission on Civil Rights," in *Civil Rights U.S.A.: Public Schools North and West 1962* (Washington, D.C.: The United States Commission on Civil Rights, 1962), pp. 29-103.

[15] Alan B. Wilson, "Residential Segregation."

Three recent analyses of the effects of racial composition on performance are far more sophisticated and complete than any of the above. These are:

1. the analysis of integration and achievement reported in *Equality of Educational Opportunity* by Coleman *et al.*[16]

2. the further analysis of these same data by McPartland and York, described in the appendices published by the U.S. Commission on Civil Rights.[17]

3. a special analysis by Alan B. Wilson of the University of California at Berkeley of data collected for the Richmond Youth Project.[18]

The first analysis, in the body of the Coleman Report, achieved statistical control of social class and racial variables by means of a regression analysis. The achievement of black students appeared to be highly related to the proportion of whites in the student body until the analysis controlled the social class composition of the school. The introduction of the school's social class composition appeared to reduce sharply the power of the school's racial composition as a predictor of achievement. The interpretation was made that white middle class children are more beneficial for black children within integrated schools than white lower class children.

The analysis, however, could not control the social class background of the individual whose achievement scores were examined and thus could not attempt to control in an important respect for both collective and individual properties. The Negroes who are achieving relatively well in schools with higher status white children may be of higher social status themselves.

McPartland and York's subsequent secondary analysis adds control of individual social background for the black population. This is the logical equivalent of our analysis in Table 5, even if only for a black sample. The original data collected in the Equal Opportunity Survey was not used entirely in the analysis of the Coleman Report described

---

[16] James Coleman, *Equality of Educational Opportunity*, p. 330ff.

[17] James McPartland and Robert York, "Further Analysis of Equality of Educational Opportunity Survey," *Appendices: Racial Isolation in the Public Schools*, II (Washington, D.C.: U.S. Government Printing Office; Commission on Civil Rights, 1967), 35-142.

[18] Alan B. Wilson, "Educational Consequences of Segregation in a California Community," *Appendices: Racial Isolation in the Public Schools*, II (Washington, D.C.: U.S. Government Printing Office; Commission on Civil Rights, 1967), 165-206.

above. Representative black subsamples were drawn for the regression analysis. The sub-samples were more likely to come from segregated schools because the black population as a whole, is found in segregated schools. McPartland and York used a multivariate analysis in which they hunted for the atypical cases of middle and lower class Negroes attending desegregated schools of varying social class composition.

The secondary multivariate analysis concerns only Negroes living in the metropolitan Northeast (they could not find cases for comparison in the other areas); there are controls for both the individual's social class characteristics and social class and racial composition of the school. Parent's education, parent's aspiration, presence of certain material possessions, and presence or absence of reading materials in the home were used in different analyses as different indices of social class. The index of the school's racial composition was the proportion of white students in the individual's classroom during the previous year. The indices of performance as a dependent variable were achievement test scores and deficiency in reading skills. The aspiration index was the aspiration to go to college as well as the presence or absence of a fatalistic attitude toward success.

The results of the analysis showed a small but consistently favorable effect associated with the proportion of white students in the individual's classroom the previous year. The differences between a totally segregated situation and a "more than half white" situation were the most consistent. The weakly desegregated classroom did not show consistently more favorable results with increasing the proportions of whites. The pattern was evident for Negroes with parents who had very little formal education as well as for Negroes with parents who had a high school education or more. Furthermore, the pattern appeared for schools with a low average of parental education as well as for schools with a higher average of parental education. When the parental education index was combined with a further index of parental aspiration, there seemed to be an even more favorable effect associated with a desegregated situation for the middle class Negro.

There are problems with the use of parental education as an index of black social class. The question on parental education suffered from non-response rates particularly among lower status respondents. Furthermore education does not seem as closely related to income and occupation for Negroes as it is for whites.[19] The analysts tried a more purely

---

[19] Walter Fogel found that the correlation between years of education and housing, income and consumption characteristics in the Los Angeles Census tracts was much stronger for whites than for Negroes. For whites, Pearson correlation coefficients between years of schooling on the one hand and housing units with

economic index such as the absence of a refrigerator in the home, but it did not discriminate among the higher status levels. When the analysts attempted to combine any two indices to balance these problems, the cases in the important comparisons were often only ten subjects or less.

Wilson's survey in the Richmond area suggests a further limitation on McPartland and York's results. Wilson's analysis suggests that some of the effect of the individual's classroom racial composition may be "washed out" by the inclusion of two new factors drawn from the earlier life history of the individual. These are (a) the IQ score on a test administered in the first grade and (b) the social class and racial composition of the individual's elementary school.

The rationale for the inclusion of early IQ scores is its reflection of the joint effects of genetic endowment and pre-school environment. There is a good deal of variation in these scores among social and racial groups in the beginning of their schooling. Unless these differences are taken into account, we may mistake the effect of continuing or later school experiences for the *initial differences* between individuals attending different kinds of schools. No set of cross-sectional data can avoid this problem.

The advantage of Wilson's longitudinal data became apparent when he controlled all the individual and school composition factors recommended in our Table 5, and in addition, controlled early IQ scores, while examining the effects of racial segregation of the individual's early and later schools. Using a test of reading achievement as his dependent variable, he found that the social class composition of an individual's elementary school is a more important predictive factor than the racial composition of an individual's previously attended school or the racial or social class composition of an individual's present school.

> This analysis shows that, allowing for variation in primary grade mental maturity, the social-class composition of the primary school has the largest independent effect upon 6th grade reading level. Among students who attended school with similar social-class composition, neither the racial composition of the school nor the characteristics of the neighborhood made any difference.[20]

Note that this particular school composition effect is not a function of the social class or racial composition of an individual's neighborhood. What does this finding suggest about the McPartland and York results? It suggests that Negroes who attended integrated schools had higher

all the plumbing, income and availability of two or more autos on the other was about .62; while for Negroes the highest coefficient was .264. "The Effects of Low Educational Attainment on Income: A Comparative Study of Selected Ethnic Groups," *The Journal of Human Resources* 1, No. 2 (1966), p. 22.

[20] Alan B. Wilson, "Educational Consequences," p. 180.

mental maturity test scores to begin with; and that this may account for their higher subsequent achievement. Curiously enough, the social class bias of I.Q. score is an advantage here, for the score is used as an important and stringent control of pre-school environmental factors. Wilson's finding that parental occupation does not clearly predict early I.Q. scores among Negroes demonstrates the need for a more stringent control of black individual's social class than the indices chosen by McPartland and York. The need for better analysis of status factors in the black population becomes dreadfully apparent. It may be more useful to conceptualize these variations as caste rather than class phenomena.

Wilson's analysis, for all its sophistication, is still a secondary analysis of collected data and suffers from the central problem of any secondary analysis. Because the survey was not designed to meet the requirements of Wilson's analysis there are frequently few or no cases in some critical comparisons. It is clear that one has to make provision ahead of time to take in a sufficiently wide geographical area to find cases for some comparatively rare instances. A most important suggestion arising from this study is the inclusion of early IQ score as an index of early home factors as well as the control of the effects of social class composition of the elementary school an individual attended if we wish to estimate the effects of integrating junior high or high schools.

There has been very little research on the last dependent variable of alienation. We found one study of the racial composition of the school attended and the probability of transfer by the principal (presumably for disciplinary reasons). Singleton and Bullock found that an individual attending a minority group high school in Los Angeles, had a much higher probability of an enforced "social adjustment" transfer or transfer to special correctional schools and camps.[21] Although we cannot tell what portion of these "social adjustment" transfers are the result of outright prejudice or cultural misunderstanding of minority group members, it is possible to infer that some portion of these transfers involve alienated youth. Thus, we have a suggestion in these data of greater alienation in students attending largely minority group high schools. Wilson finds that if Negroes or whites attend a junior high school that is predominantly lower class, they are more likely to acquire an official police record for delinquency. The relationship holds even among boys with a low achievement record (another predictor of officially recorded delinquency).[22]

---

[21] Robert Singleton and Paul Bullock, "Some Problems in Minority-Group Education in Los Angeles Public Schools," *Journal of Negro Education,* XXXII, No. 2 (1963), 137-45.

[22] Alan Wilson, "Residential Segregation," p. 200.

Once more, the social class composition appears as a factor that is very likely to be confused with racial composition.

SUBSTANTIVE CONSIDERATIONS

If the educational picture for black youth is to be successfully altered in their favor, we must move beyond the selection of variables for maximizing prediction of performance, aspiration and alienation. Even though we are not specifically studying the process by which school composition factors effect students, it is necessary to develop some conception of the important conditions of this process. With a minimum number of substantive assumptions about process conditions, we can predict that certain school settings will be more favorable than others for the black student. If our hypotheses are correct, we will have come closer to reaching a usable understanding of the phenomenon, than if we made no *a priori* assumptions or predictions and merely examined the correlations between the variables selected for study.

Assumption 1.   School composition factors take effect on the students through the medium of the school "climate," a characteristic of the organization. The concept of "climate"[23] involves at least these three factors:

1.   Available reference groups
2.   Admired and valued behavior
3.   A general morale factor

First, the reference groups available to a student in a school appear to be related to the aspiration level. Bell finds that the status of the high school reference group is a predictor of aspiration, holding constant the social class background of the student.[24] Secondly, in his book, *The Adolescent Society,* Coleman shows how much variation there is between high schools in the type of behavior (scholastic, social or athletic) considered most admirable and the consequences of this variation for social structure and behavior.[25]

The third aspect of high school climate, as we think of it, is the general school morale. Certain high schools are a source of great pride to their students, while others are viewed as a "prison" which society

---

[23] An alternative line of argument is that school composition factors take effect through organizational features associated with composition. For example, lower class schools are often highly authoritarian bureaucracies.

[24] Gerald D. Bell, "Processes in the Formation of Adolescent Aspiration," *Social Forces,* XLII, No. 2 (1963), 179-86.

[25] James Coleman, *The Adolescent Society,* (Glencoe, Ill.: Free Press, 1961).

compels its teenagers to attend. On the grade school level, Deutsch describes the variables causing a poor morale in an all-Negro grade school located in a slum area:

> Despite the seeming adequacy of the available physical facilities, in many classes . . . there was an atmosphere of disorganization, an emphasis on disciplining, minimal academic teaching, and much emphasis on "creative expression." Rarely, though, for the teacher or the administration did any activity take precedence over maintaining order, and nuclear subgroups of children in various classes preoccupied themselves with challenging behavior and disruption of any order which was obtained. The disorganization reflected a lack of motivation on the part of the pupils, and, to a lesser extent, on the part of the teachers, coupled for many of them with a cynicism as to the efficacy of standard educational procedures in this situation. Their aim was mainly to keep order, and their expectation was not in terms of the children actually learning.[26]

Assumption 2. The more homogeneous the composition of the school in either the class or the race factor, the more powerfully the climate will affect the individual's aspiration, attitude and performance. Both the highly college-oriented, totally middle class suburban school and the school in a large slum area are examples of homogeneity accompanied by a powerful climate effect of raising or lowering aspirations. Looking at one of these homogeneous schools from the student's point of view, even if he wants to be "different," there are no alternative reference groups. His peer groups share the general value system, and even the curriculum is single-mindedly constructed for the needs of the clientele. Thus a boy with hidden college potential attending a slum school has a limited choice of academic courses to stimulate him.

> Prediction 1.   Schools with a homogeneous lower class composition have the most unfavorable climate for high performance and aspiration.

Available research, reviewed above, is certainly consistent with this assumption of the underlying importance of the class factor, both in its direct effect on the individual and its indirect effect through school composition. To the already depressant effect of the lower class composition factor, this condition adds the power of homogeneity, described in Assumption 2.

> Prediction 2.   Schools with a homogeneous lower class composition and a racial composition largely black will have the highest proportion of alienated individuals.

---

[26] Martin Deutsch, "Minority Group and Class Status," p. 3.

Observers of the contemporary scene often marvel at the comparatively low level of Negro alienation, considering his previous experiences. Even so, there are still more grounds for alienation of the lower class Negro than for the alienation of the lower class white—less hope of changing one's status, a greater probability of a broken home, less hope of even minimal employment after schooling and less backing of school norms by parents.

Prediction 3.   The lower class black attending a largely black school of a homogeneous lower social class composition will have the lowest probability of high performance and aspiration in the sample.

This prediction follows from the effect outlined in the first prediction plus the further deterioration of the school climate because of the presence of a higher proportion of alienated individuals in such a school.

Prediction 4.   For a black of a given social class, all other conditions held constant, a change to a middle class school composition will be more strongly associated with a rise in aspiration and performance than a change to a mixed racial composition.

This prediction follows directly from the literature implying the effect of social class is stronger and more consistently found than the effect of race.

Prediction 5.   The favorability of a given combination of school conditions will vary with black subgroups. For example, integrated, middle class schools will be associated with a more favorable performance differential for working class black girls than for working class black boys.

Much of the literature on aspiration and performance shows sharp differences between black boys and girls. We fully expect that a rank ordering of favorable settings will differ between working class black girls and boys. Likewise, what may be a favorable setting for a black student of low IQ may be unfavorable for a black student with a high IQ. Although we are aware of the unestimated degree of cultural bias in the IQ tests, a high score is still an excellent predictor of school performance and therefore of upward mobility in our education-oriented society. We are less sure of what a low IQ score for a black student means, but it is entirely possible that a specially favorable setting can help overcome initial cultural deprivation in some of these low-scoring students.

PROCEDURE

SELECTION OF MATCHING SCHOOLS

The first step in collecting data for the cells of the research design (see Table 5) must be a decision on what constitutes a pair of schools matched in racial and social class composition. The logic of the design calls for as many matched pairs of schools as we can find within limits of time and resources. The number of cases in each cell must be large enough to stabilize the differences between cells. The operational definition of a predominantly black school or a *de facto* segregated school presents difficult problems. We can argue that a school with 70%-90% black students is predominantly black, but we frequently find that a school with only 40% black students is definitely regarded as a "*de facto* segregated*" school. If there are few Negroes in a community, but they all live in the same area and all attend the same school, the school may suffer from all the difficulties of "*de facto* segregation" even though the actual proportion of Negroes is small. In order to consider this social-psychological dimension of a school's image, we include a measure of whether or not black leaders and school personnel perceive the school as "*de facto* segregated." In addition to this criterion, we assume that a school having passed a certain mark in its proportion of black students, tends to increase that proportion rapidly as white families flee the school district or move their children into private schools. Therefore, for schools in the 30%-70% range, we look at the pattern of change in the proportion of black students in the school over the last three years. If the proportion shows a sharp growth trend, we check to see if the criterion, of perceived *de facto* segregation, is also fulfilled. Schools over 90% black are not suitable because there will not, unless it is a very large school, be enough white individuals of two different social classes to fill the cells of whites attending a predominantly black school.

In review, the definition of a "predominantly white school" is a school with less than 30% black students. If two schools fall within this definition, they are considered to "match" in racial composition. There are two alternative definitions of a "predominantly black school." One is the relatively simple criterion of a 70%-90% black racial composition. The other has three required properties: (1) 30-69% black racial composition, (2) an increasing proportion of black student population in the last three years and (3) the school perceived as "*de facto* segregated." These two alternatives are treated as equally valid bases of matching. If school A meets the first criterion and school B meets the second criterion, they are considered as matched predominantly black schools.

The design also calls for schools matched on social class composition. Distributions of the father's occupation taken from a random sampling of school record cards could be matched. Because we deal with the Negro group which is primarily working class, we need some fine divisions for matching, such as skilled, semi-skilled, unskilled and unemployed.

It is very difficult to estimate without some pilot work, just how possible it is to match the two criteria of racial composition and social class composition. If the study can be done on a wide geographical basis, the probability of finding "good matches," even though across state lines, increases. If we are restricted to one state, we may have to shift from senior high schools to junior high schools, which are more numerous, and we may have to make the definition of a match more crude. (Certain recent improvements in computer storage and search procedures increase the feasibility of this study.) Pilot work on the matching procedure is clearly the first step necessary in the study.

MATCHING INDIVIDUALS WITHIN MATCHING SCHOOLS

The next major step is the selection of individuals matched in sex, race, and social class within schools of matching composition factors. For example, from the student population of a predominantly white working class school and its mate, a predominantly black working class school, we must find pairs of students who are of the same race and sex, and have the same occupational family background but attend these two racially different types of schools. If possible, it would be desirable for these individuals to match in early IQ scores. From the student population of a predominantly white middle class school and its mate, a predominantly white working class school, we must find pairs of students who are of the same race and sex and have the same occupational family background but attend schools with a different social class composition. Since we do not expect to find black middle class schools which can be matched to predominantly white middle class schools, the matched pairs of individuals would only be used to compare a social class composition difference, given a predominantly white racial composition, and to compare a racial composition difference in predominantly working class schools. Information concerning social class composition of the selected sample's elementary school should also be gathered.

DEPENDENT VARIABLES

1. *Aspiration:* The student's aspiration can be determined by response to a written questionnaire. There are two major distinctions we wish to make in this area. One is the aspiration to

attend college vs. no aspiration to attend college. The other is a distinction between level of occupational aspiration, particularly if there is no aspiration to attend college. Because we know that many blacks drop out of school when the legal leaving age is reached and subsequently have difficulties in finding and keeping employment, we must select younger high school students to question them on their feelings about staying in school. One of the best available measures of educational aspiration is the Guttman scale developed by Wallin and Waldo in their recent study of academic aspirations and school adjustment of junior high school youngsters in the San Francisco area.[27]

Stephenson's study of ninth grade students' occupational aspirations shows the need to distinguish between student's realistic occupational expectation as compared to occupational aspiration.[28] Our questions designed to measure occupational aspiration should cover both these dimensions, but the direct use of Stephenson's questions would be inadvisable as 21% of the Negro ninth graders in his sample responded with "don't know" to his question on realistic occupational plans. This index should be developed through some pre-testing.

2. *Alienation:* In a recent study of high school rebellion, Stinchcombe[29] conceptualizes two types of alienation—expressive, a matter of verbal attitude, and open rebellion, measured by expulsion from class, and skipping school. Examples of alienated attitudes are feelings that the attendance office, the teachers and coaches are unfair, that there are too many squares in the school, and that parents feel uncomfortable at school and the PTA. These and other attitude items were designed to measure the three characteristics of the expressively alienated youngster, hedonism, negativism and autonomy from adult interference. Stinchcombe found a strong correlation between expressive alienation and actual behavioral rebellion. Furthermore, he found that open rebellion was closely correlated with a poor articulation between school experience and one's future.

---

[27] Paul Wallin and Leslie C. Waldo, "Social Class Background of 8th Grade Pupils, Social Class Composition of Their Schools, Their Academic Aspirations and School Adjustment," Cooperative Research Project No. 1935 (Stanford University, 1964).

[28] R. M. Stephenson, "Mobility Orientation."

[29] Arthur Stinchcombe, *Rebellion in a High School* (Chicago, Ill.: Quadrangle Books, 1964).

Articulation was measured by the definiteness of curriculum choice and by the belief that good grades were important to one's occupational future. It is important to note that the articulation hypothesis held strongly within the working class portion of the sample. We might include some of these dimensions of behavioral and attitudinal alienation. The two difficulties in Stinchcombe's measurement are (1) his reliance on a behavioral report of rebellion by the subject himself (and gets a fair number of "No Answers") and (2) his measures of negativism, short-run hedonism and autonomy from adult interference are from items analyzed singly. He finds that beyond the major correlations reported above, his results are bewilderingly variable. A legitimate suspicion may be held that this is due to his overly casual methods of measurement. We would need to develop a more sophisticated set of measures on a pretest questionnaire closely related to Stinchcombe's theoretical ideas and to some of his items.

An excellent measure of maladjustment or alienation from the school classroom is Wallin's scale of four items concerning the students' perception of the teacher's understanding, liking and fairness.[30] Although Wallin did not find a difference between Negro and white working class youngsters in scale score, the instrument might still prove useful for comparing the responses of youngsters from the same racial and social class background experiencing different types of schools.

A final possibility of measuring personal, psychological alienation in which the person has little liking and respect for himself is suggested by Rosenberg's seven-point Guttman scale using "contrived items," from ten items dealing with the student's sense of self esteem.[31] His scale shows correlation with measures of depression and other neurotic indicators. If a measure of potential psychological maladjustment varies with the type of school experience, we have a serious matter for further investigation.

3. *Performance:* Choice of performance measures depends upon the area covered in the study. If it is within one state, certain statewide measures currently in use by the schools will serve. If the study extends beyond a single state's boundaries, widely

---

[30] Paul Wallin and Lesley Waldo, "Social Class Background," p. 66.
[31] Morris Rosenberg, *Society and the Adolescent Self-Image* (Princeton, N.J.: Princeton University Press, 1965), p. 17.

used measures such as reading grade level probably would be more appropriate. Grades must be used cautiously because they do not capture differences between schools.

DATA ANALYSIS

With this type of study the data analysis becomes comparatively simple. One compares the direction of the difference between matched pairs of students on the several dependent variables. The strength of the design lies in its control of other important variables correlating with the dependent variables. Predictions can be tested separately for girls and for boys as well as for students testing at various levels on IQ measures. Another useful feature of the design might be the inclusion of an analysis of the effects of various attempts at remediation directed toward the culturally deprived student. If such data on the various schools in the study were collected, we could examine in the context of racially balanced or imbalanced schools the response of economically disadvantaged students with low IQ scores to special programs. This suggestion is just one example of the basic utility of a highly controlled design in survey research, where enough is known about basic correlations that will be found in the data to forsee the major sources of interaction.

A SHIFT IN TIME SCHEDULING

We have tried to illustrate some basic principles of the research method through explaining this controlled comparison survey in such detail. First, as in so many social problems, the question of a proposed manipulation's effectiveness is thoroughly tangled with the operation of closely related variables. In this particular case, the effectiveness of proposed manipulation of racial balance cannot be estimated without careful control of social class factors. We have shown the necessity for a logical analysis of the characteristics of the ideal, controlled comparison situation. In this case an integrated situation could be compared with a segregated situation and the effects estimated for comparable individuals.

Secondly, we have attempted to use the available research and conceptual literature wherever possible for defining the major concepts, for developing *a priori* predictions, for suggesting additional control variables and for measures where something is known about response patterns.

Third, we planned to devote a great deal of time and trouble to certain types of pre-testing. Note the wide, time-consuming search necessary for finding cases with the needed characteristics. Then in all the critical comparisons, we can be assured of a sufficient number of cases, carefully matched on the control variables. Also, each index of test and control variable should be pre-tested to solve problems of non-response and to find items with a sensible interrelationship.

Fourth, we looked ahead to the problems of developing explanations for the process of affecting the individual through changes in the structure variable. We did this by developing tests and planning to test certain simple theoretical ideas. We also constructed the design to stimulate speculation about the conditions under which the relationship is strong, weak, or absent.

Lastly, the need for elaborate statistical analysis of the data becomes less important when the design is built around critical comparisons. There is no need for regression analysis which uses "statistical" controls because the survey's design already has solved the control problem.

In review, we suggest a shifting of the time scheduling in the research process. More time should be spent in the conceptual analysis and pre-test phase of the research. In that way, less time will be necessary for analysis and secondary analysis of already collected data.

seven
INTERRACIAL INTERACTION DISABILITY

Despite what people often say, theories are really very practical. They provide an economical way of characterizing very complicated, concrete every-day situations. They also give us a logical way to think about these situations and their improvement, if we deem them a problem. Take, for example, the interaction between members of the white and black races, as they work together on a task—in a job, in an organization, in a school. Often there is a diffusion process whereby the social expectations of Negro inferiority infect the new work situation, when, from a rational standpoint, these expectations have no place. The whites expect the blacks to do less well; the black accepts this evaluation of his competence. There is a self-fulfilling prophecy; the whites are more active and competent in the new task; the blacks play a less active, competent and influential role. The society's real loss occurs because this process continues independently of the actual competence and motivation of the individuals. This phenomenon is called "interracial interaction disability," and it is a common element in many of the current social problems between the races.

PRODUCING EQUAL STATUS INTERACTION IN A LABORATORY

If we could prevent social expectations from infecting new tasks, we would have equal status interaction. But this is easier said than done. The practice during the recent struggle for a more integrated society has been the simple placing of more whites and blacks together in situations where the formal organization defines them as equals. In the schools, for instance, there has been strong emphasis on placing black and white children inside the same building even if a strict tracking system continues to segregate the blacks within that building. Also, there has been a great demand for hiring additional blacks on technical and white collar staffs in educational and business settings.

Although this is a first and necessary step toward a more integrated society, it often leads to friction, self-segregation, the confirmation of stereotypes each race holds for the other and the surfacing of unfavorable attitudes which were unexpressed in the traditionally unequal setting. From the standpoint of democratic values, equal status interaction where each person, regardless of race, employs his unique talents, competencies and motivation is desirable. We want a situation in which each person is evaluated strictly in terms of what he is able to accomplish towards the goals of the organization, if given the chance.

It is clear that we do not often succeed in producing what we desire. In an extreme situation like the army, where external pretenses to status are stripped away and where survival requires interdependence, we seem to see a real reduction in prejudice and the emergence of blacks as highly valued members of a team. Short of such extreme tactics, we would like to find a workable technique for encouraging equal status interaction within schools, organizations and on the job. We need a generally applicable technique which could be varied for the situation at hand, but has clear, effective principles, adaptable to the particular training problem at hand.

To arrive at these general principles, it will be easier to study an abstract and simplified version of the problem in a laboratory where we can judge the effects of several experimental manipulations. Theory becomes an invaluable help in deciding which of the infinite elements of the complex, concrete situation to capture for the laboratory setting.

APPLICATION AND EXTENSION OF STATUS CHARACTERISTIC THEORY

In this chapter we shall characterize the problem and its solution in terms of a status characteristic theory, a very abstract, logical set of ideas currently being developed by a group of sociologists at Stanford.[1]

---

[1] Joseph Berger, Bernard P. Cohen, Thomas L. Conner, and Morris Zelditch Jr., "Status Characteristics and Expectation States," in *Sociological Theories in Progress,* eds. Joseph Berger, Morris Zelditch, and B. Anderson (Boston, Mass.: Houghton Mifflin Company, 1966), pp. 29-46.

After identifying the key elements of the problem through elements of the theory, its propositions and assumptions will be used to describe the phenomenon and characterize the potential manipulation of the situation. The theory provides the bridge between the outer world and the laboratory by its selection of the important aspects for inclusion in the micro-setting and by its provision of rules of relationship between observable elements whether in the field or laboratory setting.

Before the situation can be manipulated in the laboratory setting, we need a more precise description than the rough characterization presented above. We need a description of the imbalance in the interaction between the races along the particular dimensions selected as important by the theory. Then, we will have established a basis for comparing the interaction of a group which has undergone a retraining procedure with the interaction of a group which proceeds unhindered.

If we successfully describe the imbalanced interaction pattern, we can proceed in several ways to manipulate the pattern. At least one method, Assertion Training, has been demonstrated in experimental literature, by Katz.[2] Assertion Training must be re-evaluated in our theoretical dimensions of interaction. If it produces in the key dimensions, a favorable behavior change for blacks and whites it has potential practical application outside of the laboratory setting. If, as suggested by Katz's experimentation, it produces a favorable change for blacks but also has some negative side effects on whites who do not enjoy working with newly assertive blacks, we can examine the difficulty with very little social cost and with greatly improved clarity.

If we repeat Katz's finding of negative side effects, our theory suggests alternative modes of producing equal status interaction. Once a technique is found which works safely in the laboratory and can transfer its beneficial results to interaction in different situations we can begin to move into job training and special group problem solving school tasks. We also can begin describing the effects of retraining on specially selected whites and blacks. We will know what to measure and examine in the field situation, and how to evaluate success or failure under uncontrolled conditions.

No social engineering of equal status environments will insure positive results until we have a more basic understanding of the conditions for changing the individual's sense of adequacy and changing the stereo-

---

[2] Irwin Katz and Melvin Cohen, "The Effects of Training Negroes Upon Cooperative Problem Solving in Biracial Teams," *Journal of Abnormal and Social Psychology,* LIV, No. 5 (1962), 319-25.

typical expectations within the supposedly "equal-status" situations. In other words, we claim that equal-status situations cannot be defined in terms of administrative arrangements such as busing Negro students into a white middle class school. Equal status situations must be defined in terms of a theory concerning the change that happens to individuals during the course of and as a consequence of interaction between the races.

NEGRO SELF-CONCEPT

The most typical treatment of this problem has been to define it as a problem of Negro self concept. Many studies agree that the theoretical element of Negro self-concept is central to the analysis of school maladjustment. The concept is used in a wide range of educational problems, including the analysis of the cultural deprivation and low performance of high-aspiring middle class Negro high school students. Clark cites the Negro's inferior concept of himself as the key to the problem of academic adjustment. He feels there is no solution to this problem within the framework of the de facto segregated school since it is the symbol of second class citizenship with matching expectations of inferiority.[3]

Currently, self-concept is being used to explain certain types of academically relevant behavior. For example, if a person views himself as basically inadequate, he will be unlikely to show successful striving behavior. Within the school setting, the work of Brookover and Wallin suggests that a sense of inadequacy rather than an inherent lack of ability may produce poor academic performance. Brookover finds a correlation between a student's self-concept in an academic area and his achievement holding constant his IQ.[4]

Wallin and Waldo find that both Negro and lower class white junior high school students are no more likely to complain of teachers' unfair evaluation and misunderstanding than middle class students. Rather, they are just as likely to feel that they are treated fairly. The difference between the status groups shows in the tendency of the lower status

---

[3] Kenneth B. Clark, "Educational Stimulation of Racially Disadvantaged Children," in *Education in Depressed Areas*, ed. Harry Passow (New York: Teacher's College, Columbia University Press, 1964), pp. 142-62.

[4] Wilbur B. Brookover, Ann Paterson, and Thomas Shailer, "Self-Concept of Ability and Academic Achievement of Junior High School Students," Report of Cooperative Research Project No. 845 (East Lansing, Michigan: Michigan State University, College of Education, 1962).

student to see his own capacity for academic tasks as inadequate.[5] These authors suggest that the sense of inadequacy is probably the best explanation for differentials in academic performance.

Negro "self-concept" is an extremely broad construct drawn from the work of James, Sullivan, Horney, Mead and others. It refers to the process of identity development and maintenance. Originating as a learned response to significant people in the child's life, self-concept involves both feelings of native self-esteem and feelings of adequacy at tasks. A person with a low self-concept lacks self-esteem and has a generalized sense of inadequacy.

The current use of the concept is best illustrated in a recent symposium. The line of reasoning was as follows:

> . . . in general, the environmental press of the American color-caste system tends to develop conceptions of self in Negro children and youth which result in defeated behavior as far as academic and political development are concerned.[6]

Describing this unfavorable environment in more detail at this symposium, Jean Grambs refers to the Negro's historical position in American society and to the unfavorable family situations of many impoverished Negroes in present day America.

In conceptualizing our research problem, we have rejected this umbrella-like definition of self-concept; under its shelter are gathered such diverse notions as a persistent pathological lack of self-esteem, a sense of inadequacy at specific school tasks, and a personality-culture construct of Negro character based on American history. For our purposes, one of these definitions will be more useful than others. In our case, it is particularly important to eliminate the historical element and clarify the definition of self-concept as a stable trans-situational quality of the person (the personality approach) or as a function of the expectations of others in social situations (the sociological or social psychological approach).

Because our phenomenon is one of social interaction, the most fruitful choice of concept would appear to be related to the interactionist view of self-concept, i.e., self evaluation as a function of the evaluation of others in various situations. But our idea of self-concept cannot be purely situational because we deal with the diffuse status characteristic

---

[5] Paul Wallin and Lester C. Waldo, "Social Class Background of 8th Grade Pupils, Social Class Composition of Their Schools, Their Academic Aspirations and School Adjustment," Report of Cooperative Research Project No. 1935 (Stanford, California: Stanford University, Department of Sociology, 1964).

[6] William C. Kvaraceus, J. S. Gibbon, and Jean Grambs, *Negro Self-Concept: Implications for School and Citizenship* (New York: McGraw-Hill, 1965), pp. 1-2.

of race, which provides certain continuities in many situations. Certain specific expectations such as musical and athletic ability as well as diffuse expectations of inferior performance in socially important tasks are associated with being a Negro. Depending upon the cultural meaning of various situations, different expectations will be evoked, and therefore different phases of self-concept.

Because we choose to view Negro self-concept in this theoretical light, we do not deal with the individual's perception of himself when working with members of his own racial group. He may have a very high self-concept in this context and be a very high performer in new cognitive tasks. Rosenberg's analysis of a scale measuring a clinical version of self-esteem demonstrates that a sense of adequacy and a basic sense of being worthy of love are not necessarily empirically linked. He finds a relatively small difference in the probability of having a low self-esteem score between Negro and white high school students, although he does find strong clinical correlates with score on this scale.[7]

EXPERIMENTAL EVIDENCE

The most impressive evidence for the syndrome we have termed interracial interaction disability comes from two exploratory studies conducted at a Northern university.[8, 9] Various cognitive and motor tasks were assigned to groups composed of two Negro college students and two white college students who were total strangers. During the several sessions they worked together, it was found that Negroes displayed marked social inhibition and subordination to white partners. When the teams were engaged in cooperative problem solving, Negro subjects made fewer proposals than did whites and spoke more to whites proportionately, than to each other. In the second study, Negro and white partners were matched on intelligence and made to display equal ability on certain group tasks. Negroes ranked whites higher on intellectual performance, preferred one another as future work companions, and expressed less satisfaction with the group experience than did whites.

These results suggest that interaction disability is not linked to cultural deprivation, but is a handicap observable in some middle class and up-

---

[7] Morris Rosenberg, *Society and the Adolescent Self-Image* (Princeton, New Jersey: Princeton University Press, 1965).

[8] Irwin Katz and Lawrence Benjamin, "Effects of White Authoritarianism in Biracial Work Groups," *Journal of Abnormal Social Psychology*, LXI, No. 3 (1960), 448-56.

[9] Irwin Katz, Judith Goldston, and Lawrence Benjamin, "Behavior and Productivity in Biracial Work Groups," *Human Relations*, XI, No. 2 (1958), 123-41.

ward mobile Negroes. The Negro's unrealistic estimate of his performance, more from cultural expectations rather than actual performance, is
best demonstrated by the investigation of Katz and Benjamin.[10] Here
Negro students in biracial work teams who had scored as well as their
white teammates on various intellectual tasks rated their own performance as inferior.

We have additional experimental evidence of the importance of these
cultural expectations of superior and inferior performance associated
with race in explaining behavior on intellectual tasks. Preston and
Bayton[11] found that Negro college students lowered their goal levels
when they were told that their scores on intellectual tasks were the same
as white students. They did not lower their goal levels when they were
told that their scores equalled those of other Negroes. The idea that
interaction disability can be triggered by an implied interracial comparison and an intellectual task is further supported by a study of Negroes
at a southern Negro college.[12] The task was first described as a research
instrument studying eye-hand coordination, a non-intellectual characteristic. A second set of instructions given to a different group of subjects
described the instrument as an intelligence test. Scores were markedly
lower for the groups who thought that the test measured intelligence than
for the groups who thought the test measured coordination. Both groups
were examined by a white tester. Katz, Epps and Axelson[13] also found
that Negroes scored higher on a digit symbol task under instruction
involving Negro test norms than under instructions involving white
norms, i.e., scholastic aptitude test with national (predominantly white)
college norms vs. scholastic aptitude test with Negro college norms.

Hatton's imaginative study of bargaining behavior provides further
evidence of the behavioral differences in the Negro-Negro situation vs.
the Negro-white situation.[14] Hatton compared Negro bargaining behavior
when faced with a white role player and with a Negro role player. The

---

[10] Irwin Katz and Lawrence Benjamin, "Effects of White Authoritarianism in
Biracial Work Groups."
[11] Malcolm G. Preston, and James A. Bayton, "Differential Effects of a Social
Variable Upon Three Levels of Aspiration," *Journal of Experimental Psychology,*
1941, XXIX, No. 5 (1941), 351-69.
[12] Irwin Katz, S. Oliver Roberts, and James M. Robinson, "Effects of Task
Difficulty, Race of Administrator, and Instructions on Digit-Symbol Performance
of Negroes," *Journal of Personal and Social Psychology,* II, No. 1 (1965), 53-59.
[13] Irwin Katz, Edgar G. Epps, and Leland J. Axelson, "Effect Upon Negro
Digit-Symbol Performance of Anticipated Comparison with Whites and with Other
Negroes," *Journal of Abnormal Social Psychology,* LXIX, No. 1 (1964), 77-83.
[14] John M. Hatton, "Reactions of Negroes in a Biracial Bargaining Situation."
Journal of Personality and Social Psychology, VII, No. 3 (1967), 301-06.

design needed four different confederate situations: a white confederate who was a hard bargainer, a white confederate who was a yielding bargainer, and Negro confederates who were hard and yielding bargainers. When faced with Negro confederates, Negro high school girls responded to hard bargaining techniques with hard bargaining of their own; and they responded to yielding behavior with softer, more yielding bargaining. Conditions involving white confederates brought very different results. If the white confederate were a hard bargainer, the Negro girl showed yielding behavior thus minimizing her payoff; and if the white confederate were a yielding bargainer, she became a hard bargainer, taking advantage of the situation in an aggressive fashion. This experiment shows the importance of the interaction partner's status in predicting behavior: blacks behave very differently in a "white" frame of reference than in a "black" frame of reference.

KATZ'S ASSERTION TRAINING EXPERIMENT

Katz not only demonstrated the phenomenon of interracial interaction disability, but also was able, in other laboratory work, to change the interaction patterns of Negroes when faced with whites. He further demonstrated that this experimentally manipulated change was followed by changed behavior on a new and different task.[15] Biracial dyads, composed of Negro and white Northern college students, engaged in cooperative problem solving under two experimental conditions. Under one condition, called Assertion Training, the Negro and white partner were given different amounts of information giving the Negro an easier version of the problem 50% of the time. The partners were required to reach a team decision and then announce the correct solution. Under the other experimental condition, called No Training condition, the difference in the amount of information given to the two partners did not force one of them to propose the correct solution with a high degree of confidence. The partners were always matched on ability for the task through pretesting. Under Assertion Training conditions, the Negroes and whites showed equal influence in determining the team answer. Under the No Training condition, the Negroes showed less confidence than whites in their answers and had less influence on the team decisions than whites. The No Training condition exhibits interracial interaction disability, while Assertion Training experimentally produces a more equal-status interaction situation.

---

[15] Irwin Katz and Melvin Cohen, "The Effects of Training Negroes Upon Cooperative Problem Solving in Biracial Teams."

Having artificially removed the interaction disability, Katz then examined the transfer effect on the Negro subjects of a successful experience in taking the initiative with whites. Before and after the problem-solving task, the subjects were required to guess the number of objects in some briefly presented stimuli. The procedure required each partner to guess, show his guess to his partner, make a second guess and then reach a team guess after which the Experimenter stated the correct answer. The relative amount of each partners' influence was defined in terms of the similarity between the team decision and his first guess. The influence scores of Negroes who had experienced Assertion Training showed a significant increase from pre- to post-test as compared to the influence scores of Negroes who experienced the No Training condition. Furthermore, Negroes who had undergone Assertion Training showed an increased tendency to base their second guess on an estimate of their own and their partner's previous accuracy. Negroes in the No Training condition showed no correlation between second guess movement and accuracy.

This experiment provides some basis for the theory that interaction disability can be manipulated experimentally resulting in behavioral changes in a different task. One important and disturbing finding of this experiment was that whites in Assertion Training downgraded their partner's ability and tended to reject him as a future co-worker. Katz believes these findings show that a confident show of ability by Negroes is ego-threatening to whites. An alternative interpretation is that the Assertion Training procedure, itself, is responsible for these negative feelings. If this is true we should observe the same reaction in an all-white dyad subjected to Assertion Training conditions.

DEVELOPMENT OF ASSERTION TRAINING

Perhaps the Assertion Training idea has practical possibilities for re-training Negroes and whites for equal-status interaction. Why is careful conceptualization and laboratory study needed, rather than simply using the technique on the population of a newly integrated school? The first problem emerges immediately. Katz' work was concerned with college Negroes while the newly integrated school deals with a younger population with a lower social class average background. What crucial adaptations of the procedure are needed for the non-college younger population? What type of a task should the retraining procedure involve? Is there any assurance that we will not change inadvertently some critical feature embodied in the problem-solving task Katz used? Beyond the problem of the proper conditions for the new technique's application is the problem of possible hostile, anxious reactions from the whites. Would this reaction be magnified in a field setting? Certainly we need to know more about the causes of this reaction and ways to prevent it before using it in a relatively uncontrolled situation.

A major criticism of previous experimental work is the tenuous connection between the theoretical concepts used as explanatory factors and the actual experimental demonstration of the phenomenon. The work of Katz and his associates demonstrates the phenomenon we have described, but the bewildering array of concepts used in their conceptualization of the problem does not allow progress towards an understanding necessary for cumulative work. To illustrate: In the report of the experiment on behavior and productivity in bi-racial work groups[16] the following concepts are listed as factors governing the social behavior under study: (1) non-hostile withdrawal; (2) hostile withdrawal; (3) inhibition of hostility; (4) substitute locomotion; (5) feelings of inadequacy. These concepts are defined by other complex ideas involving a host of implicit assumptions. Without further explanation or deduction the authors present their predictions, claiming they follow logically from propositions about these five factors: (1) Negroes will direct a larger proportion of their non-hostile behavior to whites than whites will direct to Negroes; and (2) Negroes will communicate less than will whites. The reader does not understand how these predictions are derived. Nor does he know if all these concepts are necessary for understanding the problem.

After introducing their predictions, Katz, *et al.,* describe an extraordinarily complex experimental design involving more than interracial interaction. Additional factors such as the effects of group rewards as opposed to competitive individual rewards, and the effects of group prestige are built into the design. These additional factors have no intrinsic relation to the concepts the authors have introduced; no propositions are given to explain their relationship to the initial concepts. They do not clarify the phenomenon.

The introduction of too many theoretical concepts interferes with systematic reasoning and forces us to guess intuitively how to develop Assertion Training as a practicable technique. If we wished to vary the re-training manipulation, we would have to employ a trial and error method of operating, unless we first find some set of guiding concepts, assumptions and propositions.

---

[16] *Ibid.*

STATUS CHARACTERISTIC THEORY

It is our opinion that Katz' conceptualization is inadequate for understanding this phenomenon and developing the conditions for change. We feel that a more heuristic conceptualization can be based on a few ideas from the current theoretical work of Cohen, Berger and Zelditch.[17]

Status characteristic theory explains the way in which prior status factors determine the emergent power-prestige order in a task-oriented group. Race is viewed as a diffuse status characteristic for the following reasons: (1) there are different states of the status characteristic (black and white), and associated with these states is a system of beliefs involving valued and disvalued characteristics (for example, the Negro is associated with many characteristics such as laziness and rowdiness, etc.)[18]; (2) a state of a diffuse status characteristic also involves expectations or beliefs about the performance of actors from a given state in a wide range of situations. Associated with the Negro race is society's general expectation that he will do less well in a wide variety of valued tasks.

Using the basic concepts of diffuse status characteristic, evaluation and expectations, we would describe the dynamics of interracial interaction disability in the following manner:

1. The Negro is in the less valued state of the diffuse status characteristic of race.

2. Associated with the Negro state of the diffuse status characteristic is the general expectation that the Negro will be inferior to whites on cognitive tasks.

3. Whites hold the expectation that Negroes will be inferior on cognitive tasks.

4. Negroes know this expectation, and it molds their own self-expectations of inferior performance and influence; i.e., Negroes have a low self-concept in tasks involving whites.

5. The low self-expectation of Negroes generates low aspirations.

6. When low performance occurs it confirms the white expectations for the Negro and the Negro's expectation for himself.

---

[17] Joseph Berger, Bernard P. Cohen, and Morris Zelditch, Jr., "Status Characteristics, and Expectation States".

[18] Otto Klineberg, ed. *Characteristics of the American Negro* (New York: Harper and Row, 1944), pp. 1-22.

7.   When Negro high performance occurs, it is not recognized (see the Katz, Goldston and Benjamin experiment reported above).

MOVING INTO THE LABORATORY

The status characteristic theory will be useful in the design of descriptive and experimental studies concerning interracial interaction disability because it systematically states the structural conditions for the process of diffusion. The statement constitutes guidelines for the invention of the laboratory task. Only if we meet these boundary conditions will inter-racial interaction disability occur: (1) We need a task with differing outcomes having differing evaluations (such as winning or losing a game). This task must require the actors to consider each other's behavior and must be sufficiently ego-involving so that the participants are committed to its successful completion. (2) There must be some element of competence demanded in the task which is perceived as instrumental for its successful outcome. (3) The participants in the task must be differentiated on a diffuse status characteristic involving both specific and general expectation states. (4) There must be no basis for discrimination between the participants other than the diffuse status characteristic. (5) The needed competence must not have been previously associated with or disassociated from the diffuse status characteristic.[19]

The theory of status characteristics aids us also in selecting aspects of the process and its outcome for description and manipulation. If there is a diffusion from the racial status characteristic, we will expect to find the resultant power and prestige order on the experimental task reflecting the power and prestige order of Negroes and whites in the larger society. This idea is based on previously accumulated experimental evidence and on the present experimental work testing the theory's basic propositions. We are directed toward the particular dimensions of interaction such as having certain *action opportunities*, (as when the individual is asked a question). We should also consider individual contributions to the task, known as a *performance output*, and *unit evaluations*, which are assumed to be a necessary consequence of the conditions named above, i.e., the nature of the task forces people to evaluate each other's performance. The distribution of all these dimensions is the "observable power-prestige order."[20] We can expect to find a high intercorrelation between the

---

[19] Joseph Berger, *et. al.*, "Status Characteristics and Expectation States," p. 41.
[20] *Ibid.*, p. 43.

components of this order; the rate of positive evaluations should correlate positively with the rate of performance output, etc. Furthermore, these indices of interaction should correlate with measures of the actual influence over the final group decision.

This description of relevant dimensions tells us the type of indicators of interaction we will need to construct. We can then describe the phenomenon in terms of these indicators. We also are provided with specific predictions for comparing white and Negro behavior in the group. We will expect rates of action opportunities and performance outputs to be greater for the actor who has the high (white) state of the diffuse status characteristic and to whom competence in the new task is therefore attributed. The theorists specifically have made a prediction for the racial case:

> . . . over a period of time in which they are engaged together in a task, a given Negro subject will, on the average, receive fewer action opportunities from a given white than a white will from a given Negro.[21]

Because we want to examine the continuation of the process over a period of time, we will expend more effort in constructing good indicators of interaction dimensions than in constructing indicators of influence over decisions. Our task should produce data of the desired variety. It is extremely difficult to find a task producing data for strong indicators of all the dimensions of the power and prestige order at once. Therefore, the task will be designed to highlight the giving of action opportunities, performance output and unit evaluation.

The theory can handle the possibility that Assertion Training produces anxiety and hostility in whites. If we conceive of Assertion Training as altering the expectations of the Negro so that he does not feel less competent at a new task in which he faces whites, we produce an imbalanced situation.

"Definition 2.2 A status structure in S is balanced if and only if every relational unit in it is balanced."[22] The expectations held by the whites of a lower competency for the Negro will not be matched by a similar expectation by Negroes who have been successfully trained. Thus, although the theory does not give a behavioral prediction of the consequences of experiencing imbalanced status structure, we will not be surprised to find increased tension in the whites.

---

[21] Joseph Berger, Bernard P. Cohen, Thomas L. Conner and Morris Zelditch, Jr., "Status Characteristics and Expectation States: A Process Model", in *Sociological Theories in Progress*, eds. Joseph Berger, Morris Zelditch, and B. Anderson (Boston, Massachusetts: Houghton Mifflin Company, 1966), p. 47.

[22] Joseph Berger, *et. al.*, "Status Characteristics", p. 39.

Clearly, the remedial procedures should be designed to achieve a new status structure balance. We might try a general disassociation of new cognitive tasks from the diffuse status characteristic of race, or an alteration of the general expectations held for Negroes by themselves and by whites. In other words, remedial work will probably have to be done not only for the minority group but also for the whites. If some version of Assertion Training is introduced as a practical remedial technique in a high school setting, it is possible that the resulting hostility and tension in the whites could produce a severe social problem, confirming the Negro's worst fears of retaliation. Until there is a basic understanding of the phenomenon, it is unwise to generate concrete suggestions in such a sensitive area.

Because we wish to study and manipulate a more life-like, relatively free-flowing interaction situation, we are forced to move beyond the present development of the theory. Present status characteristic theory deals with highly controlled laboratory situations. For example, the theory does not as yet specify the conditions under which the diffusion process can be prevented or interrupted. We will have to experiment with manipulating the various dimensions of interaction for this purpose. The theory does not specify for our case how the process of diffusion develops through the distribution of action opportunities to the differential distribution of influence. The present process model uses a more restrictive situation than ours. Lastly, the theory does not specifically help in the choice of dimension indicators such as "giving of action opportunities." Yet, with this theory, we are able to think about experimental alternatives for a long projected course of studies far more effectively than we could if we merely used *ad hoc* bits of knowledge from social psychology, psychology and sociology.

STUDIES IN PROGRESS

DESCRIPTION OF INTERRACIAL INTERACTION DISABILITY

The first phase of this research is beginning now at Stanford's School of Education.[23] We have run nineteen groups of junior high school boys. In each group there were two black and two white boys, matched on an index of social class background, adjustment to school, and level of aspiration. The boys had never seen each other before. They were re-

---

[23] This research is supported by an NSF Grant—GS 1833.

quired to work as a team on an experimental game developed expressly for this study. The game requires the group to make fourteen decisions about which way they will proceed on a game board. Having decided on direction for each turn, a die is rolled by the Experimenter; and the group score is determined by the addition or subtraction of score points on the square the playing piece lands.

The score is cumulative; and the subjects are informed of the highest score that a group has ever earned (a fictional number). The subjects are instructed that this is a game where not only luck is involved but also strategy. If the group chooses certain paths, they will receive a higher score but will risk never reaching the goal and thereby losing everything. The "hot paths" on the game board have a higher probability of reaching the goal but the possible points to be earned are low. The subjects are informed of these possibilities. After reaching a decision, they place their playing piece which shows the Experimenter their decision.

The game is thoroughly ego-involving and rarely fails to provoke some lively discussion and disagreement between the participants. They will sometimes discuss at length the relative merits of one member's suggested path. Although they rarely run down another member's decision overtly, they use the technique of counter suggestions which are incompatible with a strategy they find unacceptable. Thus the design features encompass a new task without previous status associations—a task which has a favorable or unfavorable outcome where the participants feel it is important to do well, and are forced to take each other's behavior into account. Because the subjects do not know each other and because they come from similar social class backgrounds and have similar adjustments to school, there is no basis other than race or observed competence at the task for the assignment of expectations.

A T.V. camera filmed the group as they played the game. The videotapes were scored in terms of observation categories based on status characteristic theory. Both black and white observers were trained to be highly reliable on the following observation categories:

1. Performance Output (a speech relevant to the task)

2. Action Opportunity (some action, requiring response, from another person, such as asking a question)

3. Negative Evaluation (disagreement, giving a counter suggestion, running down another person)

4. Positive Evaluation (agreement, praising, building up another's status)

The observer records who makes a speech, what kind of a speech it is (which of the four categories) and who is the recipient of the speech. A record is kept of the color of each of the actors.

These observation procedures are related somewhat to the Bales' method of scoring small group interaction; they are actually combined Bales' categories, but the unit of scoring is an uninterrupted speech rather than a single thought. Also, although the categories are mutually exclusive, they are not exhaustive.

An additional measure of influence is taken from the videotape records. A record is made of the number of unique suggestions concerning moves on the game board each member contributes. A second influence measure records the member whose suggestions actually become the group decision.

Analysis of the descriptive data confirmed the predictions derived from status characteristic theory. White subjects were more active than black subjects and were more likely to occupy first and second ranks on number of acts initiated. White subjects made more successful influence attempts than black subjects. The indices of influence and activity were positively related.

Our conclusion from this analysis was that our laboratory task was a suitable instance of the operation of diffuse status characteristics. In addition, careful clinical studies of the videotapes gave the necessary understanding for the construction of Assertion Training designed to alter the expectations of the participants.

This description of the pattern of differences in interaction behavior serves as a baseline situation. We assume that the diffusion process operates without interference, if we "allow nature to take its course."

PHASE 2: EXPERIMENTAL REMOVAL OF INTERACTION DISABILITY

In our experimental phase we are attempting to interrupt the process of diffusion. In our first experiment Negroes receive a simplified form of Katz's Assertion Training; i.e., we increase the competent performance output of the Negroes. By giving them better information, we increase the possibility that they will make an active and important contribution to the group task. We attempt to manipulate competence in a task where a group of junior high school boys, working together, build a crystal radio set from printed directions and instructional films. Assertion Training consists of a special videotape administered to certain black subjects while they handle and practice with actual sets. The film is constructed especially for motor and non-verbal learning. The whites and all subjects in control treatment view a videotape offering less useful information in a more verbal and conventional, professorial style. As in the development of the experimental game, the task must have the features required by the theory. In this treatment, however, the task attempts may not be purely verbal. Physical attempts to solve the construction problems are counted as "performance outputs."

The effects of this experimental treatment are checked by our observation categories to see if the performance output of blacks receiving training actually increases when compared to blacks receiving a control treatment. The control treatment has the same cooperative problem-solving task; the amount of information given to blacks and whites is held equal.

The transfer effects of the training are ascertained by the game interaction situation described in the first phase. The boys play the game before and after the treatment session. This way we are not only able to see if there is some change in behavior, but also we are able to examine the pattern of change through several different dimensions.

TABLE 6

EXPERIMENTAL DESIGN

Experimental Group			Control Group		
Pre-Test	Assertion Training	Post-Test	Pre-Test	Control Treatment	Post-Test
Inter-action on Game	Blacks see a more helpful instruction film	Inter-action on Game	Inter-action on Game	Blacks and Whites both see less helpful film	Inter-action on Game

Comparisons will be made between pre- and post-tests for experimental and control groups. Comparisons will be made between the post-test results for the two groups. In the control group, the two experiences of uninterrupted status diffusion should cause the post-test interaction to be slanted noticeably according to racial expectations. In the experimental group, the Negro interaction pattern should be altered by the Assertion Training experience.

There is one additional control group in which the pre-test is omitted. In this way we can examine the transfer of the Assertion Training effects when the subjects have had no prior opportunity for the diffusion of status characteristics which, we hypothesize, occur in the first round of the game. The behavior of this control group in the game will be compared to the behavior of the Assertion Training Group in the post-test.

In the post-test situation we predict that the whites will show the status imbalance by increasing the tension in their response when their expectations for lower performance levels from the Negroes are violated. We also expect an increase in the negative evaluation category.

Such results would indicate that Assertion Training must be counter-balanced by Tolerance of Assertion Training for whites. For example, if whites were faced repeatedly by assertive, competent Negroes, or if we formulated a training procedure to demonstrate that color is unrelated to performance on new cognitive tasks through the retraining of the least assertive white and the least assertive black from the first round of the game, we might be able to interrupt the diffusion process for both races.

This is the strength of the theory as an aid to experimentation. Katz had to use an *ad hoc* interpretation to handle the anxiety and hostility of whites when faced with assertive Negroes. Status characteristic theory implies that the interaction process is a product of the expectations for self and others in both races. To achieve a new, balanced status structure, we must contemplate altering the expectations of both status groups. Knowing how participation in interaction differs for the two races, and having some idea of the development of the process, we should be able to generate further experimental ideas of how and when to interfere in the diffusion process.

There are a whole series of possible experiments implied for developing an effective retraining procedure and examining the types of situation to which retraining effects will transfer. Soon, it should be possible to examine the transfer effects in complex field situations such as work and school situations.

FIELD APPLICATIONS

It would be foolish to assume that all Negroes are in need of Assertion Training, or that all whites are in need of Tolerance of Assertion Training. The theory only specifies that when the task has certain characteristics and there is a status difference between the participants, the power and prestige order will be a function of the participants' status. It does not say that the effect of the status difference will be observable in each participant. Some blacks will be unaffected by the presence of whites, and some whites will be unaffected by the presence of blacks. This may be because some blacks and some whites are very inhibited in any group, while some people of both races would be very active in any group working on this task. We would not be at all surprised to find that some individuals were not very much changed by any single simple training experience. In these initial studies we are describing and attempting to manipulate the effect of the situational variable of status on a group of people unselected in terms of any general "group activity" tendency.

As we prepare to move into a field situation, there are several different directions in which to proceed. One is suggested by the above discussion; we would like to develop a set of diagnostic procedures with which we can discover the population most likely to benefit by Assertion Training. If we find a group of generally inhibited and group-shy people, on whom the training is not effective, some other retraining may be in order. Also such a finding suggests that the original theory needs modification for these special conditions. People who would ordinarily participate in our task with competence and interest in a single-race group but are markedly inhibited in biracial groups, are those for whom the training should work most effectively.

Another important direction is the study of transfer from the tasks within the training setting to biracial tasks in the real world. An ideal setting for such study would be where a new biracial task is about to be introduced. Theoretically speaking, changing behavior in a long-standing biracial task where diffuse status characteristics have been operating for months (such as a typical integrated schoolroom), should be much more difficult than changing the behavior of complete strangers in a new task.

Examples of such situations are the current programs upgrading adult skills such as from nurse's aide to registered nurse or teacher's aide to teacher, or trainee in an "Equal Opportunity" industrial training program for skilled workers.

An ideal natural set-up for field experimentation would be the selection of an experimental and a control group from nurse's aides who are being retrained as registered nurses. The effect of Assertion Training in the experimental group could be compared with the effect of a control treatment. Here the transfer of training would be examined in behavior on-the-job as the newly trained nurse interacts with others in a group of registered nurses or on a nursing team.

All these training programs hope to produce workers who will enter into their new occupational status and into any group problem-solving without disabilities in working with white people. The adaptation of Assertion Training to an adult population and a technical task, should not be too difficult with the help of theoretical guidelines for task construction.

SUMMARY

There is a good deal of intrinsic interest in manipulating the biracial setting for educational purposes. But temporarily ignoring this prospect, this chapter illustrates the ways in which the theory helps. A ready-made theory has helped to choose elements of the original problem situation for translation into the laboratory, has aided in the logical development of the description and manipulation of the phenomenon in the laboratory, and has helped us to move into the field setting.

If we are successful in moving through all these stages of the research process, we will be able to give the "practical" and down-to-earth advice which the practitioner wants. This practicality would not be possible without the underlying process of abstraction.

eight
STATUS AND POWER IN THE ELEMENTARY CLASSROOM

In the first section of this book, we mentioned the lack of fresh remedial suggestions for educationally disadvantaged children. In this chapter we will try to demonstrate how a fresh look at the phenomena of concern—the depressed area classroom—and a fresh analysis, using available theoretical framework, can lead to a whole group of suggestions which may remedy the situation. We must examine the action process of the classroom more generally than piecemeal approaches such as reforming curriculum, teacher training, and school organization do. Our approach is more *selective and abstract* than many of the available approaches. We chose to consider only certain aspects of the educational process and to conceptualize the ways in which they act upon each other. If we have ignored something vital, our basic propositions should not hold under certain conditions of empirical testing. If we have included enough factors and have some good theories about their relationship to each other, we have the basic framework for constructing *many different* innovations. Our innovations, in turn, may be evaluated in terms of the factors selected in the basic conceptualization.

The conceptualizations developed in this chapter are less advanced than the theoretical framework for interracial interaction disability presented in the last chapter. They are at a more primitive stage, where we still must decide which theoretical framework will be the most suitable. Whatever our choices, certain theoretical modifications will be necessary to handle the phenomena which are crucial to the practitioner. We are exposing the act of considering various theoretical possibilities in the development of explanatory models for phenomena observed in poor urban classrooms. Through this we hope that the reader will

118

realize that these explanations are the result of a patch and fit operation between the critical features of the phenomena and the available theoretical propositions.

CHANGING PRESENT METHODS

We have stressed the selection of a phenomenon for study as the first step in an action research project. When a social problem has many interlocking features, it is helpful for the researcher to re-consider the site of the difficulty. The researcher should put aside preconceived ideas of reform. If we begin with an assignment to reform someone or something, we are likely to recommend changes which concern only one variable and ignore the others. Basically, there is a pious hope that reform of one feature will fix up what else is wrong or at least will not be negated by interlocking factors.

We will take as an example of a widely "viewed-with-alarm" social problem, the self-contained classroom filled with low status children and a single teacher. The situation is easy to criticize. There are claims that the teachers are incorrectly trained, that the children are not prepared for the classroom experience, that the environment of the street culture is not supportive, and that the organization of the school and its relation to the parents is somehow wrong. The problem is defined by questions such as: "What is wrong with this teacher's attitude?"; or "What curriculum approach would really produce results with these children?"; or "What would happen if parents really had some say in the running of the school?"

The innovations resulting from these questions have one factor in common. They are tied to the current conventional organization of the process of education. Innovations typically concern changing teacher training, dramatically altering the curriculum, introducing team teaching and teacher aides, or strengthening the role of the parents through a community-school approach. We are not questioning the effectiveness of these innovations. We are merely pointing out that they all begin not with a new examination of a phenomenon, but with all the traditional predispositions of persons and organizations who have been involved in the educational scene for a long time.

There are hidden limitations in using the conventional categories as beginnings in experimentation with the school. Putting the major problem briefly, no one (both practitioners as well as researchers) really believes a socially significant degree of change can be achieved through the alteration of only one variable in a multi-causal situation. Even if a "magic teacher" is created who is endowed with lengthy and expensive special training, she is likely to be overwhelmed by organizational features of the working situation in the urban school. The most exciting parent-school community approach may fail because of a dull, conventional curriculum, and unenlightened teachers. Conversely, the most exciting and relevant curriculum can fail in the hands of teachers who believe that the children are "ineducable" and only can be kept safe and amused by the new materials.

This piecemeal approach to reform involves improving each of these variables, one at a time. When all are improved, it is felt that the end result will be a sharp improvement in performance. If these variables really are interdependent, changes in different factors operating in the classroom will not necessarily result in improvement. The change made in one factor may well be incompatible with the change made in another factor. For instance, school organization may change in the direction of subdividing the teacher's task into routine specialized duties, while teacher training may produce "master teachers" who expect to have generalized responsibility for decision making concerning the children delegated to them. Also, extremely active parents who interfere with the teaching process, are not compatible with a teacher trained on a highly "professional" model.

Let us try a different approach to the elementary school classroom with low-status children. As a beginning we shall select some major variables which may have an effect on the children's observable behavior. We will miss much that can be said about the children, the teacher and the school, but we will have a potential explanatory system, focusing explanation on the interaction between the teacher and the child. Concern shifts from wanting to know what reformation is needed, to understanding how variables come to work jointly on the child. The research question becomes: "What is a plausible way to account for some of the major observable behaviors of the child in the classroom situation?"

The explanatory model we will develop now is in its crudest form. The major task of rationalizing the model in terms of available sociological theories remains to be done. The most exciting feature of this model is its ability to generate suggestions for change that include interlocking features of the school organization, the teacher, and the child. Of course, the quality of the suggestions for change is dependent upon the outcome of the research on the propositions generated from the model. If the basic interlocking ideas of the model are empirically verifiable, then it is possible to estimate how changes in the system are likely to effect other features.

A FRESH LOOK AT THE CLASSROOM

In creating an explanatory model, to be perfectly honest, one does not survey the available descriptive studies unimaginatively and passionlessly. The beginning is often some challenging event or observation. One wonders endlessly why certain events occur, while reading and listening to the current observers. Then, often rather suddenly, a possible explanation, accounting for multiple observable features, suggests itself.

In our case, the history of these ideas began with observations of all-black, privately sponsored schools. In most of the schools we have seen, read, or heard about, neither the curriculum nor the approach to teaching differs radically from conventional public schools. There is, however, a dramatic difference in morale and behavior. There is a heightened sense of purpose and activity differing sharply from that of the public schools.

How can we explain the fascinating contrast between behavior in the "black power" setting and behavior in the low-status public school setting which may be an unintegrated Negro school? This noticeable difference in behavior and attitude may result from many different causes, depending on your behavioral science training or your ideology. A psychologist may say that the "black is beautiful" idea causes an improved self-concept which results in an increased willingness to try to succeed. A black militant may say that only black people know how to educate black children and that in the absence of hated whites everything improves automatically. A sociologist may say that these children believe that they will benefit directly by the education they are receiving. They are surrounded by adults, coming from their own socioeconomic and racial background, who believe that they will learn a great deal and therefore will have a promising new future. Everyone who works at a school of this sort holds this belief firmly.

The sociological view is, surprisingly enough, not only a good characterization of "black power" schools, but also an equally adequate characterization of a wealthy suburban school. It is *not*, however, a good characterization of an urban school filled with low status children. Descriptive studies tell us the key features of the urban slum school classroom. We must find an explanation that accounts for some of the observable differences between the "black power" setting and the depressed area public school setting.

Passivity. In slum schools, where the military discipline theory of school administration is in practice, good control in the classroom is maintained at all costs. Teachers are evaluated on their ability to keep the classroom quiet and apparently busy. Miscreants are suspended; students usually are found in their chairs; teachers do most of the talking. Observers watching the children in this situation report that although they are quiet, they are also "tuned out" on education. Their minds and emotions are certainly elsewhere.

Incompetence.   The low status student in the urban school frequently does very poorly at school tasks. He suffers from a sense of inadequacy at these tasks. He believes that the evaluations he receives are fair, but he is inadequate (the characteristics of a low academic self-concept). He is on a starvation diet of success experiences. Observation of these children suggests that some take refuge in a "feigned stupidity" to avoid the punishment of further evaluation following earnest effort.

Powerlessness.   The students have no say in the formulation of class-room goals. The curriculum, having been created for a more academically oriented middle class client, is not important to what they value in life. The teacher constantly is concerned with discipline; i.e., putting the students under stringent control and keeping them there. Some teachers appear to give up and allow the children to do as they wish. This does not increase the child's sense of control over his environment. Parents do not feel they have any effective means of influencing the school situation. It is not surprising for Coleman to find that children of low status minority groups especially are likely to report that they feel unable to control their own environment.[1]

In some of the poorest urban areas, the children also are truant a good deal of the time. Many of them engaged in illegal activities to acquire the things they want by the only means available to them. School for these children is a custodial institution that they are forced to remain in until they can drop out.

POWER AND PAYOFF MODEL

If we focus on the interaction between the teacher and pupil while comparing the nature of the relationship between the urban slum school and

---

[1] James Coleman, *Equality of Educational Opportunity,* 320. For other descriptive studies, see: Martin Deutsch, "Minority Group and Class Status as Related to Social and Personality Factors in Scholastic Achievement;" Paul Wallin and Leslie Waldo "Social Class Background of 8th Grade Pupils;" William Kvaraceus, *Negro Self Concept.*

the suburban middle class school, we can create ideas possibly explaining some of the observed differences in behavior. We will begin with the sense of powerlessness and the passive brand of incompetence.

We shall assume that teaching is an interactive process between teacher and child, strongly conditioned by two situational variables: the nature of the task that has been set and the organizational features of evaluation and control. In the conventional classroom authority and control are vested in the teacher, and the teacher exercises this authority through evaluation of the child.

STATUS SPACE

Comparison of the status space between teacher and child in the middle class and lower class case is very instructive. For the middle class child, the teacher is of higher status by virtue of age and organizational position, not by virtue of race or social class. This is also true for the relationship between teacher and pupil in the "black power" schools. In the lower class case there is great space between the teacher and the child, the teacher is of higher status by virtue of age and organizational between teacher and child are of the diffuse variety[2] such as race and social class which may infect new situations with expectations of inferior competence taken from the general societal principal of superior and inferior expectations for high and low status people.

The greater difference in status between teacher and child yields an hypothesis explaining the greater expectations for incompetence held by both role players in the urban slum school. This difference alone would cause us to predict that teachers would think that the low status slow learners had little possibility of improved performance on new tasks. Furthermore, we would predict that the youngsters themselves do not expect to do well on new school tasks introduced by the teacher. Yet we have not as yet satisfactorily explained the power problem.

MOTIVES AND GOALS

To explain the feeling of powerlessness, we must focus on the children's motives and goals as they undertake the difficult tasks of learning. Why do children labor in school? Because of the intrinsic interest of the school work? They may work for the warm approval and positive evaluation (grades) that come from the teacher and their parents. But even middle class children not receiving good grades do not appear to give

---

[2] See discussion of Berger, Cohen and Zelditch in Chapter 7.

up, but rather continue to work anyway. If a middle class child is asked why he works in school, he is likely to say that he wants to learn something so he can become a smart man with a nice job. He not only has the short-range goals of a positive evaluation, but also the long-range goals of success in American terms. In sociological terms, he internalizes the goals of the society. Even if he can't verbalize, he has confidence; he feels that as an educated man with a good job, he will receive his share of the material rewards of society.

The teacher, for this middle class child, is a *means* to the end of achieving long-range goals. Grades, to him, signify his progress toward these goals. Even if the middle class child receives poor grades, he still may hope realistically for a successful outcome. His mother will help him at home; his father will hire a tutor; he will be sent to a special reading school or even shifted to a private school with smaller classes where he can succeed academically. If he doesn't have the grades needed for a good college, he will be sent to some college that will accept his performance level. Evidence on this last point is abundant. He is not completely dependent on the teacher's power of evaluation for a successful outcome of the immediate schooling task or the long-range schooling process.

Lower status parents and children also aspire to college and a good job, more than middle class people suppose. How can this goal be achieved through the educational setting (almost the only path to a middle class job) when the rate of failure is so high? Many minority group children continue to show high aspirations and college plans in spite of obviously unsatisfactory academic work. They know, in one sense, that they cannot achieve their goal, but they also realize that their other alternative is to give up hope for a future.

The official value system of the school tells the low status child that he can achieve long-range cultural goals by hard, perseverant work in the classroom. He agrees that education is terribly important to his goal in this society. He also perceives: (1) his own persistent academic failure; (2) very few other students in his school achieving success through scholarship; (3) many adults like his parents who have worked hard all their lives with no visible success; (4) teachers who would be very surprised if he showed any radical improvement in schoolwork. Why do we find it so hard to accept that the children of these schools often simply disbelieve the official value system?

Children appear to be shockingly accurate about their own future. Teachers, such as Job Corps personnel who work with drop-outs, have observed that it is often the brightest black youngster who leaves at the earliest opportunity, having perceived no reason for further efforts.

As the slum child acquires serious doubts about his chances of advancement through the educational process, he is confronted with alternative means for acquiring success. In his neighborhood, the successful people are the pimps, the "numbers" men and the prostitutes. They acquire the things that most Americans want. It takes a very myopic moralistic point of view to avoid concluding that the child realizes that there are means outside of the school to achieve long-range goals. The official value system of the school does not admit the existence of these alternatives because they are "unthinkable." This type of thinking makes the school's official version of the future all the more unrealistic and unbelievable to the child.

The middle class child sees the teacher as a means to an end. The low status child cannot believe realistically that working with the teacher will accomplish long-range goals. If the teacher is not seen in an instrumental light, the child's choice becomes one of working for the teacher as an end in itself; or ignoring school and withdrawing into the means-end chain provided by street culture.

Young, enthusiastic teachers, working in these schools, often comment on the extravagant loyalty and love that low status pupils sometimes show them. They report on the children's efforts to please them. These are children working for the reward of approval and love from the teacher as an end in itself. How specific and personal this source of motivation is becomes clear when these same young teachers complain, "But after they leave my classroom, they slip right back to their lackadaisacal ways. They seem too dependent on my being there. How can I persuade them to work for some other teacher?"

The differences we have discussed between the middle and low status cases can be diagrammed as follows:

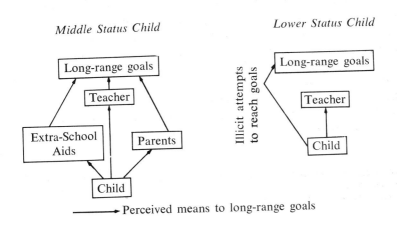

Middle Status Child   *Lower Status Child*

Perceived means to long-range goals

The unbroken arrow of the diagram denotes a perceived relationship of behavior to long-range goals. The middle status child sees his teacher, his parents and extra-school resources as helping him to achieve desirable goals. The lower status child does not perceive his teacher in an instrumental fashion but as a dead-end relationship. Illicit means are those observable and open to him for the achievement of his goals.

EVALUATION

The process of evaluation is critical to all our theoretical ideas of how passivity, powerlessness and incompetence can dominate the behavior of so many children in the classroom. There are several alternative ways of considering the evaluation process. One is derived from status characteristic theory and the other is derived from the Scott-Dornbusch theory of authority and evaluation in an organizational context.[3]

If we use status characteristic theory, we stress that, because of the operation of a diffuse status characteristic process, grades are used, not as a diagnostic tool of progress, but as a confirmation of the teacher's low *general* expectations for the student's competence as a human being. In terms of our long-range goals, these low evaluations also are evidence that there is little chance of short-term or long-term success in the schooling process. The severe differences in diffuse status characteristics and the low probability of success the student sees in cooperating with the teacher are proposed as the underlying causes of passive, incompetent behavior and the sense of powerlessness. Behavior will continue in a passive and incompetent mode as long as this process continues uninterrupted.

As an alternative, the Scott-Dornbusch ideas provide a very appealing mode of abstraction, particularly for studying the rejection of school, or dropping out, and low self-concept aspects of the children's behavior. In this theoretical framework, we would view the child as an organizational participant who cannot maintain his desired level of evaluations because the evaluator (teacher) has implicitly set unattainable standards. In theoretical terms, the child lacks the facilities to perform at a level high enough to receive satisfactory evaluations. Translated into educational terms, the child lacks the middle class behavioral traits, vocabulary and cultural background necessary for success in a conventional curriculum.

---

[3] W. Richard Scott, Sanford M. Dornbusch, Bruce C. Busching, and James D. Laing, *Organizational Evaluation and Authority,* Technical Report No. 17 (Stanford, California, Stanford University, Laboratory for Social Research, 1966).

Scott and Dornbusch predict the outcome of this instable authority structure. The actor is likely to either lower his desired level of evaluation causing the evaluations received to be more compatible with his desires or leave the authority system. This is a promising explanation for lowered levels of aspiration in some children and continuing high levels of aspiration in other children who leave school by dropping out, playing truant, or mentally leaving the system although physically sitting in the classroom.[4]

The questionnaire responses of low status high school students show feelings of powerlessness and failure in the school setting even though the students tend to maintain the aspirations for conventional success symbols. It is not surprising that observation of these students in school yields statements about their passive and absent-minded response to schoolwork and the teacher, alternating with inexplicable bursts of hostility. The contradictions built into this double position are almost more than a person can live with.

If these patterns of ideas contain the beginning of an effective explanation, then we can expect to find that certain relationships will remain when we manipulate these two features of the classroom: the evaluation process and the successful result in terms of short-range goals. The removal from the teacher-child interaction of the conditions which set the diffuse status characteristic process in motion is the first step. Changing the teacher's role as evaluator, should decrease passive and incompetent behavior. If we build into the classroom tasks the accomplishment of satisfying short-range goals, we should increase the student's willingness to work in that setting toward both short and long-range goals. His accomplishment should give him a greater sense of control over his fate or a greater feeling of power. Using the Scott-Dornbusch theory and building tasks in which the child can attain desired levels of evaluation, should reduce the probabilities of lowered aspirations and mental or physical drop-out.

Experimentation and innovation based on this explanatory model would alter the nature of the classroom task, the manner in which tasks are selected as personal goals, and the evaluation of the tasks. Increased power for the elementary student translates into a series of experiments with the following concepts: (1) an increase in his choice of his own goals; (2) an increase in the probability of receiving favorable evaluations; and (3) a new style of evaluation which is specific to his per-

---

[4] We are grateful to Albert Bergeson for the development of this identification of instable authority structures in an unpublished memorandum.

formance on a single task rather than a diffuse judgment from a high status figure of his general worth or worthlessness.

CHANGING THE CLASSROOM TASK

If the low status child does not believe he can achieve success at educational tasks, he cannot be brainwashed and forced to learn basic intellectual skills taught in a conventional manner. We suggest that he may acquire a desire to learn some of these same skills if they are part of the means for a much shorter ranged goal which he has selected himself. His power might be increased further if he could choose which of a number of tasks was most suitable for his present interests. He probably would choose that task in which he felt he had the greatest chance of competent performance. This choice would increase our chances of producing a success experience.

A perfect example of this unconventional mode of education is the experience of a Job Corps teacher who had a youth who did not want to do anything about his illiteracy but desperately wanted to drive heavy equipment. He was allowed to avoid the reading class and to enter the "heavy equipment course," although the heavy equipment course demanded the ability to read. Soon, he returned to request aid in learning to read only the introductory manual. The teacher taught only for this one very short-range goal; and the pupil returned repeatedly for more assistance, gradually acquiring a general skill in reading. By allowing the student to control and choose for himself and by making the educational activities strictly relevant to the student's goal, this teacher probably accomplished the teaching of reading skills far more quickly than by the conventional method.

With the younger child there is the increased problem of confusion and anxiety arising from being forced to make a choice. No doubt, techniques would have to be developed to assist the child in learning how to handle the problem of choice. There should be no problem in inventing entirely new curriculum tasks involving basic skills but directed towards the child's own goals rather than the required level of skill for a particular age group. Although we are not curriculum experts, we cannot picture an elementary school child refusing the chance to have a pet mouse in school if he will learn how to observe, read the directions on care and feeding, and measure out the proper food for the animal.

Many children like to build things that will work. If the task does not specify only one acceptable mode of solution, many children who may not be academically inclined, will be able to reach an acceptable solution. We are not implying a "keep the children busy and happy" routine; we are suggesting a carefully designed choice of tasks involving a wide range of competencies that are demonstrably useful in life and some academic skill training which is a part of these tasks.

If we are correct in assuming that the child does have long-range success goals, and we act to provide success on short range goals, we can predict that his willingness to attempt new tasks which he feels lead to long-range goals will increase. For example, he may work at the speaking and writing of formal English as a necessary skill for his long range goals since his expectation for a successful outcome has been increased.

REDUCING TEACHER POWER

Our ideas of underlying process suggest the removal of the evaluation function from the hands of the individual classroom teacher in the depressed urban setting. The status space between teacher and child is too great to permit the child to understand helpful evaluation as a limited, constructive message about his current work. There is too great a chance that the teacher's low general expectations for the child will be translated into a low expectation for self by the child. Low evaluations received from the teacher are taken as evidence of incompetence at the most general level by the child.

This line of thinking is not unrelated to the current attention given to changing teacher expectations derived from the work on the self-fulfilling prophecy done by Rosenthal and Jacobson.[5]

We are looking at the same phenomenon, the teacher's damaging expectation resulting in lowered performance. The key difference in our approach is the imbedding of this expectation phenomenon in a theoretical process. The theoretical framework generates many ideas for altering the working of the process. Rather than changing the teacher's thinking, we can remove the process of evaluation from her hands and place it in the hands of people or activities which do not involve low expectations for the child's performance.

Currently, there are alternative approaches for reducing the teacher's power in this classroom situation. In some community school programs, the teacher's power is reduced greatly by the potential sanction of the parents. In other urban schools the teacher's power is greatly reduced by the students' overt threats and hostility. The teacher in this setting

---

[5] Robert Rosenthal and Lenore Jacobson, *Pygmalion in the Classroom* (New York: Holt, Rinehart & Winston, Inc., 1968).

often is burdened with a large class including pathologically hostile students. She is not given the support to maintain any type of authority. Although these two situations reduce the power of the teacher, the students will not increase their activity nor become more self-assured and competent. Our set of ideas would suggest that undermining the teacher's authority will not have desired effects, nor will arming the teacher with greater resources and support. Rather, we must direct our attention to altering the process of evaluation and expectation. If we do alter the process of evaluation by removing it from the teacher, we will have a teacher with reduced power, but we will also have some desirable results in terms of student behavior.

ALTERNATIVE MODES OF EVALUATION

There are ways to evaluate the outcome of educational tasks other than a teacher's tests and grades. Some tasks may have evaluation built into them. For example, a radio crystal set will work only if the directions have been followed correctly. Many tasks combining mechanical and reading skills have this character.

Secondly, evaluation may come from peers who have decided to reach an agreement or accomplish some goal, in small work groups within a classroom. Some low status children, in educationally disadvantaged schools have written their own texts or rewritten textbooks to suit themselves. In these group activities evaluation is found in the peer members. Although small work groups have been advocated for the classroom for many years, the depressed area urban school usually is last to use these techniques. If the products of the small groups are "individual" reports which are then graded in a conventional manner by the teacher, the evaluation function really has not been shifted. The purpose of the activity has been defeated.

To develop this line of innovation, a major value and a major technical problem must be overcome. First school personnel are extremely anxious to have the individual's work evaluated. They are dissatisfied if an individual contribution cannot be assessed because it is inextricably linked to the group product. The technical problem is the need to insure that peer group evaluation is not merely the influence of the boldest student who does the most talking. The teacher's role is a very difficult one; without doing the evaluation herself, she must teach the group as a whole to evaluate each other on objective grounds.

A third possible way to alter the evaluation function of the teacher is to change her role into various components, each of which would be carried out by different people. A teacher aide could be helpful if that teacher aide's role were carefully defined to include social-emotional elements and real teaching function. Most teacher aides now do routine duties; and the teacher's power of evaluation is left undisturbed. If the teacher's aide, who usually comes from the same social class and racial background as the students could do some evaluating of the child's performance in conference with the child, we would have constructed a better status situation for the child. Theoretically, he should be more able to accept evaluation as a helpful, specific comment from an adult of his own social background. Older students might be used in the same way.

Lastly, some mechanical aides, such as computer-assisted instruction, take the burden off the teacher as evaluator. These machines evaluate the child as he progresses. They adjust their pace allowing the child to maintain a reasonable success level. The exact meaning a machine-as-evaluator has in the child's mind, is unknown. The social meaning the children assign to the machines is a critical research question because of their sudden widespread use. We do not know what the child may think the machine expects of his performance or whether he receives the evaluations in an emotionally neutral and specific way.

WHAT IS LEFT OF TEACHER'S ROLE?

With such a change in the evaluation function, can the teacher still play an expert, professional role? The teacher who can retain power over the children only through his power to punish with low grades and his power as a generalized social judge, is not a "master teacher." The limited role that we propose is the very essence of expertise based upon authority through knowledge. It is not easy for a teacher to avoid interfering with the child's choice of goals and still guide him in the art of making choices. What ordinarily happens is an unconscious imposition of his unconscious middle class goals (not really educational philosophy) on a group of children. The children understand that without changing their values to match those of the teacher, they will not be acceptable. A sophisticated variety of teacher training which enables the teacher to avoid requiring the child to identify with her value system for rewards, must be evolved.

This new teacher role would not resemble the diffuse emotional style common to elementary school teachers. Many idealistic, young teachers working with the disadvantaged attempt to solve status problems by causing the child to work for the teacher from sheer love and loyalty. Many current crash training programs deliberately develop this line of action. They select physically attractive and imposing young college graduates and place them in the classroom without much formal training. The teacher is to be so accepting, empathetic, and understanding that the children will learn from sheer love for the teacher. There are several serious problems in this technique.

Will this affection transfer to the child's next teacher? According to all reports—probably not. It may be dangerous to the child because the love relationship implies identification and he has to shed his culture to become similar to his teacher.

Identification with the teacher is more suitable in the middle class school or in the "black power" school. In the low status public school with a middle class teacher, the child finds he cannot shed his own values. If he does, he may develop a case of self-hate. We cannot afford to neglect the socio-emotional side of the child who often needs emotional support. Some emotional support might be highly specific and given by clinical experts. More practically, teacher aides recruited from the neighborhood may be able to give love and emotional support to a wide range of children—para-mothers in the classroom. In this way, the teacher's role is restricted but sophisticated. She is not the child's mother, but she is a pleasant and rewarding person to work with. The whole emotional character of the relationship is more controlled and disciplined than the role recommended in many current training programs.

The training for a teacher working in this kind of a newly structured teaching situation would have to include the following:

1. Training in providing the structure needed by the lower class child to avoid anxiety and distractibility

2. Training in teaching choice behavior to children who have had little practice in choosing goals

3. Anthropological and clinical training in cultural nuances to avoid the unconscious devaluation of the child

4. Training in small group work where the teacher avoids the evaluation role but insures that objective standards of evaluation are used by the peer group

5. Training in the flexible handling of curriculum, blending elements of basic academic skills into the experiences that the child receives from the tasks he has chosen.

6. Administrative training in handling the allocation of roles to assistant teaching personnel.

The teacher training program these pre-requisites imply would be a program very different from the usual series of courses. Many of these are specific clinical skills which would have to be practiced in the class-room under expert guidance.

Such a program would not be conceivable without supporting changes in the range of classroom tasks available to the teacher. He cannot be expected to develop all these new tasks himself. We need curriculum researchers, who are more sensitive to the different interests and typical problem-solving styles of low status children, than the curriculum de-velopers we now have.

MOVING FROM IDEA TO INNOVATION

The innovations suggested above may not seem particularly original to people who have read and studied widely in the field of teaching the disadvantaged. The end-product of our study of process is unusual because of the range of variables that we suggest are involved. Beginning with a reexamination of the classroom and the construction of a possible explanatory model, we reached the recommendations concerning the organization of the school, the curriculum and the role of the teacher.

To use these ideas, we need more confidence in the propositions under-lying this model. The model must be rationalized in theoretical terms for its basic propositions to have a clearly testable form. The most difficult theoretical problem for solution is the interrelationship of ex-pectation theory and the existence of short-range and long-range goals. After these propositions are developed, they should be tested by some basic experimental work.

If we have some confidence in our pattern of explanatory ideas, we could experiment with the innovations derived from them. Because the conceptual and experimental base exists, this research phase would have to use specially formulated control groups rather than a conventional control group in which the particular treatment is simply withheld. Our control group would hold constant all conditions known to affect the dependent variable and vary only in one critical innovative feature. The control group would not be a conventional urban classroom which would be compared to a classroom innovation involving all the latest ideas. Neither the experimental nor the control group would be similar to a conventional classroom. Both would be essentially innovative, but, as one possible example, the process of evaluation would occur in a different manner in the experimental group than in the control group.

The dependent variable would not be standardized achievement tests but rather, success at particular tasks, the voluntary choice of these tasks, and persistence at similar new short-range tasks and dissimilar new long-range tasks.

IMPLICATIONS FOR ACTION RESEARCH

The research process just discussed has all the distinguishing features of the approach to action research suggested in this book: (1) abstract characterization of an underlying phenomenon; (2) formulation and testing of propositions based on these abstract ideas; (3) innovation *based* not on artistic intuition, but on the manipulation of the studied process and (4) the testing and evaluation of these innovations *within* the framework of ideas concerning the process.

This chapter examined innovations, the modes of research designed to test innovations, and the breadth of the ideas for change developing from a new explanation of the classroom's problems. This approach contrasts with the more conventional approach of reform through the invention of new ways to continue the traditional functions such as teacher training, curriculum invention or school administration. Although the course recommended here may seem impractical because of its abstract quality and its demands for an early research phase, it is felt to be more practical in the end result because of its capacity for handling the interrelated problems of a field setting. It is more creative because of its capability of generating innovations that cannot be reached through other modes. Lastly, it is more practical because it presents new approaches to the constant problem of evaluating the effectiveness of new techniques.

nine
THREE PITFALLS

During several years of working with practitioners who are learning how to do applied educational research, we have found several persistent problems with the approach to research. We have mentioned these in previous chapters. Now we would like to give detailed attention to the undesirable consequences of these errors in formulating the research problem.

The examples are again taken from the area of race and education, but the problems apply to most "action research." The first problem concerns the difficulties of choosing race as a research concept in formulating the problem. This exemplifies the more general difficulty of choosing a level of abstraction which is suitable for a scientific enterprise. It further exemplifies the difficulty in distinguishing between a problem suitable for an historical approach and a problem suitable for a scientific approach.

The second danger concerns the fallacy of assuming that all members of a certain group suffer from the same problem. This difficulty originates in the non-statistical way we think about social problems. We assume that all slum children are pre-delinquent, or that all Mexican-Americans have not assimilated American culture, or that all "hippies" are middle class rebels. This assumption produces very poor applied research if not corrected in the very early phases.

The final and greatest danger concerns the problem of ideology and values. Frequently our values and emotions cause us to begin work on the problem. Our values certainly help us to choose the desirable goals for behavior change as a product of our research. But these same values can cloud our judgment of the study's design and the interpretation of the evidence. The applied researcher working on urgent social action problems, must take elaborate measures to protect himself from himself. These measures include stating his hypothesis so that it is possible to prove himself wrong. The method of translating the problem into abstractions is an aid to cool and careful formulation. It is not desirable for the researcher to make observations himself. It is usually better to rely upon people who do not know the hypothesis. Finally, the inclusion of people in his research staff who do not have his value system is essential. They can challenge him and force him to explain his own assumptions, thus helping him to remain intellectually honest.

RACE AS A RESEARCH CONCEPT

Given our approach to applied research on "race," race is an unsuitable term for a research conceptualization.

Suppose that you, as an educational researcher, are concerned about the educational problems experienced by people who are identified as "blacks" or "Negroes." You may have a strong idea of the source of some experienced difficulties; or you might actually know how to improve the situation. To use the research frame of reference described in the preceding chapters, you must ask yourself two basic questions:

1. What phenomenon do I wish to study?
2. Of what more general concept or theory is this phenomenon an instance?

The term "race" is a poor answer to either of them.

For the first question, "race" as a general word is really not a specifically observable phenomenon. Just what observable phenomenon do you want to discuss? In education, we typically are concerned with a set of experiences or behaviors occurring frequently in the racial group— economic, occupational, educational, psychological experiences or behavior. A phenomenon is not a concrete thing in and of itself, but refers to aspects of reality as they are experienced or sensed. To answer the first question, then, we must specify whether we are speaking of the behavior of black children in the school setting, the behavior of white personnel toward black children, feelings of anger and hostility, occupational experience of the college-educated black person, or the rising political efficacy of the black community in influencing the schools. In a statement of the research topic of the phenomenal level, the word "race" undergoes an initial transformation.

In answering the second question, "race" undergoes an even more radical translation. Upon close analysis, the second question moves us into the scientific realm. The term "race" becomes a historical rather than a scientific concept. The words "concept" and "theory" in the second question refer to abstractions that are free of time and place connotations.

Neither the word "race" nor terms such as "segregation" or "black militancy" are free from temporal and geographic change. A study of recent history in this country shows the change in the meaning of race with the passage of historical time. Now that we have experienced a rising tide of black militancy does being black mean the same thing as it did back in pre-militancy days? Does being black mean the same thing now that the number of Negroes employed in white collar and professional jobs has skyrocketed? In a geographical dimension, does being black in Brazil where skin color is not so closely associated with social status, mean the same thing as it does in this country? Obviously, the answer to these questions is, "No." A scientific concept is unique because it is free of time and place connotations; race is an historical term precisely *because* it has very different social and psychological meanings at different times and places.

Vital historical studies can be and are being made of "black power." But black power or race is not a subject for scientific study until it is identified as an instance of some more general, time-free, place-free concept. For example, you might identify the current successful influence on schools of the black power groups as an instance of a general theory concerning pressure groups and their ability to effect social change. Or, the researcher might identify the racial characteristic as a status characteristic. In both cases, there is a transition to a level where propositions exist without reference to time and place; i.e., without reference to any particular pressure group or any particular status characteristic.

The advantages, as we have stated before, of achieving this level of abstraction are that: the scientific theory can reveal unsuspected features and relationships of the phenomenon under study; and the researcher may be able to state with some confidence the conditions under which your manipulations will succeed.

These advantages must be weighed against certain disadvantages, because the process of abstraction is not a simple procedure. For one thing, the researcher may incorrectly identify the phenomenon involving blacks as an instance of the more general concept. He might, for example, choose to study black behavior as an instance of low-status behavior, only to discover many blacks behave in a way that, according to the theory, is "high-status." There are other problems concerning the choice of the particular theory he follows since none of the available theories are well developed or verified. Sometimes, there is no relevant theory, and he must develop abstract concepts and invent propositions.

Unfortunately, there is no other known way to acquire the power that a scientific level of theory can supply for prescribing solutions to problems under a specifiable set of conditions. Furthermore, as he answers the key questions previously proposed the researcher should lose the concept of "race" as a basic term in his research formulation.

The client or student who is forced to transform the initial idea of race into an observable phenomenon and then into a more abstract level, is relieved of the emotional cloud surrounding the word. In these times of racial crisis, researchers, regardless of their own color, are generally so emotional about the term, that it is difficult for them to think in a rational and rigorous fashion. A research formulation becomes a polemic or an involved justification for one's own past behavior. A good question to ask the would-be researcher, struggling with the initial formulation, is "Can you describe the phenomenon without once using the words connoting race?". At first, he may resist the request because it seems absurd to ignore the word that implies his motivation for the study.

However, what emerges after a struggle is most rewarding. With clarity, and less emotion, he will describe to you the observation causing him to feel that there is a problematic situation. For example, the school administrator, troubled by his relationship to blacks in his community, tells you that these are a people distinguished by the frequency of mistrust of the school; i.e., they don't trust the school to act in their child's best interests. Further queried, he abstracts this phenomenon as an example of feelings of mistrust and futility, perhaps some type of social alienation. It becomes apparent that: (1) not all black parents feel this way; (2) parents who mistrust may not be the same parents who feel futile; and (3) some non-black parents may feel the same way with the same consequences of a disturbing relationship to the school. Now, he has begun to analyze the problem in a way that will permit a reasonable research task.

THE GROUP FALLACY

Many educational innovations make the error of identifying their population as all the poor black and brown people. Their reasoning seems to develop from comparative surveys where the probability of certain problems is much greater for this group than for a white middle class control group. There are many studies showing statistically significant differences in characteristics which are thought to promote school success between racial and socioeconomic groups.

Although it is obvious to many readers, it is still necessary to make the following statement. Significant differences do not prove that a neighborhood population of low-status people or families who enroll in a Headstart program *necessarily exhibit* the particular deficiency or educational problem you want to correct. These descriptive studies may show significant differences but they also show that the distributions of the compared populations overlap; i.e., some low status individuals have less of a problem than some high status individuals. Actually, low status populations in these comparative studies frequently show greater *variability* than high status populations. As a further complication, previous literature gives no basis for the expectation that the existence of educational gaps or lacks tends to gather together in the same individual. Rather, it appears that different problems are found in different children.

In a study of early math skills such as counting, matching, and recognition, Leiderman found that: (1) not always the same children failed on the various tasks she gave them, (2) one of her "disadvantaged" samples was often indistinguishable in performance from her middle class control group, and (3) the disadvantaged group usually was outstanding for the variability in performance scores between individuals.

> The variability in performance within the disadvantaged classes was shown to be consistently very large. The variability between classes of disadvantaged children was also found with regularity. Both of these trends demand a more careful look at the factors affecting the individual's performance and make imperative a caution in grouping the findings of a number of classes on the basis that they are all composed of children who can be described as disadvantaged.[1]

Treating a group identified solely by its color and economic status is futile. Yet we often select all the children from a poor neighborhood for Headstart programs or other remedial educational treatments. We simply assume that there is no particular harm from being exposed to unnecessary educational measures. Perhaps, if we knew exactly what the individual were lacking, we could supply that skill effectively in Headstart programs or in the kindergarten year. At the present time, we may miss

[1] Gloria Leiderman, William Chinn, Mervyn E. Dunkley, *The Special Curriculum Project: Pilot Program on Mathematics Learning of Culturally Disadvantaged Primary School Children*, SMSG Reports, No. 2 (Stanford, California: Stanford University Press, 1966), p. 80.

the level of effectiveness because we distribute our remedial measures indiscriminately.

In designing an innovative program or an educational research project concerning the disadvantaged, the learning difficulty that the treatment is designed to remedy must be described first. Then a diagnostic survey must be done to find the children who are experiencing the particular learning difficulty. If you have a solution for children who suffer from lack of auditory discrimination, then you first should be able to identify those members of the population who give evidence of the problem.

If a typology of learning difficulties could be constructed, it would yield surprising results. Children who show a specific difficulty would come from many different racial and economic backgrounds. By stereotyping a racial or ethnic group in terms of learning difficulties we make a great mistake. A good demonstration of this result is a little study of learning readiness in two well-to-do Jewish groups in Brooklyn who are descendants of Jewish groups in very different foreign cultures. One group showed sharp deficiencies in tests of learning readiness in comparison to the other group, although both had excellent economic and social backgrounds.[2]

Once the learning difficulty has been identified, the problem's focus rapidly shifts from one of Headstart programs for poor black neighborhoods, to a program of diagnosis and treatment for children of all types who probably will experience some difficulties in learning. Depending upon the outcome of specific studies of diagnosis and treatment, the timing of the training programs may vary from preschool, to kindergarten, to later years.

We must separate those recognizable learning difficulties from the more general problems arising from broad social factors such as "a sense of powerlessness." These latter problems will not be solved by considering the child a jigsaw puzzle and trying to discover which pieces of necessary training are missing. Both approaches obviously are necessary. The major difficulty with the current approach is that it is used to solve both kinds of problems—the specific learning difficulties and the larger social problem of the black's status in relation to the formation of school policy—with one relatively simple, general approach to "all the black children in the community."

THE NOBLE SAVAGE FALLACY

There has been a certain tendency in the literature written for people working with the "disadvantaged," to glorify what is essentially lower

---

[2] Morris Gross. *Learning Readiness in Two Jewish Groups: A Study in "Cultural Deprivation"* (New York: Center for Urban Education, 1967).

class culture. Writers who become incensed over the lack of understanding middle class teachers show for lower class children, try to make the practitioner understand that the child simply is not a collection of missing middle class virtues. He has strengths of his own which should be appreciated by the teacher. He should not be changed into something which he is not. He should be cherished and protected for what he is.

Certainly there is room for training these teachers in the area of understanding and accepting the contemporary behavior of the children. The difficulty arises when the teacher sees the child as unchanging and does not expect any growth or change to occur. The child can be enclosed in this romantic pigeonhole of the "noble savage" and not let out again. If you are busy appreciating his own cultural qualities, you may expect him to become a replica of his parents.

But, we are in a period of very rapid social change. Just as we cannot judge students in good-bad terms because of culturally conditioned behavior, we cannot prescribe what they will become. Lower class black culture, itself, presently is undergoing dramatic changes with the rediscovery of African elements and the growth of militancy. Some blacks are adopting this new culture. Some are not, but are taking advantage of new economic opportunities to become middle class in culture and economic style. If we adjust perfectly to present-day lower class black culture, we may discover, ten years hence, that the culture we have "adjusted to" is an anachronism among black people.

In doing applied educational research, it should be possible to select some more relevant concepts than "lower class culture" and "strengths of the lower class child." We need concepts that do not imply these underlying value problems. More valuable, it would seem to us, is a careful study of the characteristic problem-solving styles of these children as they work individually and in groups. With this information in mind, we might consider new curricula based upon these particular skills. Perhaps the same intellectual problems we traditionally solve verbally, can be solved in more than one way. Another closely related and useful concept is the insuring of successful experiences that are relevant and important for both the school and the child. With successful experiences in a properly designed curriculum, the child may be encouraged sufficiently to attempt the more typically verbal curriculum, such as the learning of standard English. If we avoid crippling him by failure experiences and teach him how to solve difficult problems, he may take any stance toward black culture that he wants. If he wants to be in the forefront of the militant movement, he will know how to acquire relevant skills. If he wants to become a white collar worker who behaves as a "white" he can pick up as many elements of middle class white culture as he wants. And if he wants to move to a high status occupation, but wants to remain outside of the white middle class culture and within some new kind of proud black culture, he can do that too.

This is basically a value problem. If one takes a stance of cultural pluralism, one does not imprison the child within his own culture. Instead, one accepts certain cultural features while capitalizing on educationally relevant cognitive styles to achieve educational goals. This should provide the child with the flexibility to move culturally and occupationally within the society. We want whites and blacks to feel reasonably at home in each other's world, losing some of their present fears, guilt and hostility. We are hopefully not engaged in either the futile attempt to preserve lower class black culture as it stands today or in designing blacks who feel compelled to "turn white."

The white researcher should ask himself some very searching questions concerning his ideas for the desirable changes in the behavior and attitudes of black children. It is easy for the white, even with the belief in cultural pluralism but without having examined the hidden values in his work, to try to change blacks into whites, counting all changes in this direction a victory. Likewise, it is easy for the black researcher to try to change all black children into staunch militants. Perhaps the value position that this volume has articulated is that the role of the educational system is not a total institution producing a pre-designed end product. Our society is changing much too rapidly both economically and culturally for that kind of value system. Rather, our goal might be to do whatever is necessary to help children acquire skills, patterns of thinking, and a sense of personal efficacy which allow them to make important value decisions for themselves.

Selected Bibliography

Bell, Gerald D. "Processes in the Formation of Adolescent Aspiration," *Social Forces,* XLII, No. 2 (1963), 179-186.

Berger, Joseph, Bernard P. Cohen, and Morris Zelditch, Jr., "Status Characteristics and Expectation States," in *Sociological Theories in Progress,* Joseph Berger, Morris Zelditch, and B. Anderson (eds.). Boston: Houghton Mifflin Company, 1966, 29-46.

Berger, Joseph, Bernard P. Cohen, Thomas L. Conner, and Morris Zelditch, Jr. "Status Characteristics and Expectation States: A Process Model," *Sociological Theories in Progress,* Joseph Berger, Morris Zelditch, and B. Anderson (eds.). Boston: Houghton Mifflin Company, 1966, 47-73.

Bloom, Benjamin S., Allison Davis, and Robert Hess. *Compensatory Education for Cultural Deprivation,* New York: Holt, Rinehart & Winston, Inc., 1965.

Brookover, Wilbur B., Ann Paterson, and Thomas Shailer. *Self-Concept of Ability and Academic Achievement of Junior High School Students.* Report of Cooperative Research Project No. 845. East Lansing: Michigan State University, College of Education, (1962).

Cain, Glen, and Harold Watts. "Problems in Making Inferences from the Coleman Report," Discussion Paper, Institute for Research on Poverty, University of Wisconsin, (1968).

Clark, Kenneth B. "Educational Stimulation of Racially Disadvantaged Children," *Education in Depressed Areas,* Harry Passow (ed.), New York: Teacher's College, Columbia University Press, 1964, pp. 142-162.

Coleman, James. "Equal Schools or Equal Students," *Public Interest,* I, No. 4, (Summer, 1966), 70-75.

Coleman, James S., Ernest Q. Campbell, Carl J. Hobson, Alexander M. Mood, Frederic D. Weinfeld and Robert L. York. *Equality of Educational Opportunity,* U.S. Department of Health, Education and Welfare, U.S. Office of Education. Washington: Government Printing Office, 1966.

Coleman, James S. *The Adolescent Society.* Glencoe: Free Press, 1961.

Deutsch, Martin. "Minority Group and Class Status as Related to Social and Personality Factors in Scholastic Achievement," *Society for Applied Anthropology Monographs,* No. 2 (1960).

Fogel, Walter. "The Effects of Low Educational Attainment on Income: A Comparative Study of Selected Ethnic Groups," *The Journal of Human Resources,* I, No. 2 (1966).

Gilbert, John and Frederick Mosteller. "Educational Data Open Questions," *Science,* CLVI, (June 16, 1967), 1435.

Gist, Noel P., and William S. Bennet. "Aspiration of Negro and White Students," *Social Forces,* XLII, No. 1 (1963), 40-48.

Gordon, Edmund. "Characteristics of Socially Disadvantaged Children," *The Review of Educational Research,* XXXV, No. 5 (1965), 377-378, 385.

Gross, Morris. *Learning Readiness in Two Jewish Groups: A Study in "Cultural Deprivation,"* New York: Center for Urban Education, 1967.

Hatton, John M. "Reactions of Negroes in a Biracial Bargaining Situation," *Journal of Personality and Social Psychology,* VII, No. 3 (1967), 301-306.

Holloway, Robert G., and Joel V. Berreman. "The Educational and Occupational Aspirations and Plans of Negro and White Male Elementary School Students," *Pacific Sociological Review,* II, No. 4 (1959), 56-60.

Jencks, Christopher. "Education: The Racial Gap," *The New Republic,* CL (October 1, 1966), 21-26.

Kaplan, John. "New Rochelle: A Report to the U.S. Commission on Civil Rights," *Civil Rights U.S.A.: Public Schools North and West 1962,* Washington: The United States Commission on Civil Rights, 1962.

Katz, Irwin, S. Oliver Roberts, and James M. Robinson. "Effects of Task Difficulty, Race of Administrator, and Instructions on Digit-Symbol Performance of Negroes," *Journal of Personal and Social Psychology,* II, No. 1 (1965), 53-59.

Katz, Irwin, Edgar G. Epps, and Leland J. Axelson. "Effect Upon Negro Digit-Symbol Performance of Anticipated Comparison with Whites and with Other Negroes," *Journal of Abnormal Social Psychology,* LXIX, No. 1 (1964), 77-83.

Katz, Irwin, and Melvin Cohen. "The Effects of Training Negroes upon Cooperative Problem Solving in Biracial Teams," *Journal of Abnormal and Social Psychology,* LIV, No. 5 (1962), 319-325.

Katz, Irwin, and Lawrence Benjamin. "Effects of White Authoritarianism in Biracial Work Groups," *Journal of Abnormal Social Psychology*, LXI, No. 3 (1960), 448-456.

Katz, Irwin, Judith Goldston, and Lawrence Benjamin. "Behavior and Productivity in Biracial Work Groups," *Human Relations*, XI, No. 2 (1958), 123-141.

Klineberg, Otto (ed.). *Characteristics of the American Negro*, New York: Harper & Row, 1944.

Kuhn, Thomas S. *The Structure of Scientific Revolution*, Chicago: University of Chicago Press, 1962.

Kvaraceus, William C., J. S. Gibbon and Jean Grambs. *Negro Self-Concept: Implications for School and Citizenship*, New York: McGraw-Hill Book Company, 1965.

Lazarsfeld, Paul. "Evidence and Inference in Social Research," *Daedalus*, LXXXVII, No. 2 (1958), 99-130.

Leiderman, Gloria, William Chinn and Mervyn E. Dunkley. *The Special Curriculum Project: Pilot Program on Mathematics Learning of Culturally Disadvantaged Primary School Children*, SMSG Reports, No. 2, Stanford: Stanford University Press, 1968.

Leeson, James. "Some Basic Beliefs Challenged," *Southern Education Report*, II, No. 9 (1967), 3-6.

————. "Questions, Controversies and Opportunities," *Southern Education Report*, I, No. 3 (November-December, 1965), 7.

Levin, Henry. "What Difference Do Schools Make?" *Saturday Review* (January 20, 1968), 57-69.

Levin, Henry, and Samuel S. Bowles. "The Determinants of Scholastic Achievement—An Appraisal of Some Recent Evidence," *Journal of Human Resources*, III, No. 1 (Winter, 1968), 3-24.

McKissick, Floyd. "Is Integration Necessary?" *The New Republic*, CLV, No. 23 (December 3, 1966), 33-36.

McPartland, James and Robert York. "Further Analysis of Equality of Educational Opportunity Survey," *Appendices: Racial Isolation in the Public Schools*, II. Washington: U.S. Government Printing Office, Commission on Civil Rights, 1967, 35-142.

Michael, John A. "High School Climates and Plans for Entering College," *Public Opinion Quarterly*, XXV, No. 1 (1961), 585-595.

Moynihan, Daniel Patrick. "The Negro Family: The Case for National Action," *The Moynihan Report and the Politics of Controversy* Lee Rainwater and William L. Yancey. Cambridge: The M.I.T. Press, 1967, pp. 39-124.

Neimeyer, John. "Some Guide-Lines to Desirable Elementary School Reorganization," *Programs for the Culturally Disadvantaged.* Washington: U.S. Government Printing Office, 1963, 81.

Pfautz, Harold, William Sewell and Leonard Marascuilo. "Review Symposium," *American Sociological Review,* XXXII, No. 3 (1967), 475-482.

Popper, Karl R. *Poverty of Historicism,* New York: Harper & Row Publishing Company, 1964.

Preston, Malcolm G., and James A. Bayton. "Differential Effects of a Social Variable Upon Three Levels of Aspiration," *Journal of Experimental Psychology,* XXIX, No. 5 (1941), 351-369.

Rosen, Bernard. "Race, Ethnicity and Achievement Syndrome," *American Sociological Review,* XXIV, No. 1 (1959), 47-60.

Rosenberg, Morris. *Society and the Adolescent Self-Image,* Princeton, N.J.: Princeton University Press, 1965.

Rosenthal, Robert, and Lenore Jacobson. *Pygmalion in the Classroom,* New York: Holt, Rinehart & Winston, Inc., 1968.

Schrag, Peter. "Why Our Schools Have Failed," *Commentary,* No. 3 (March, 1968), 31-38.

Scott, Richard W., Sanford M. Dornbusch, Bruce C. Bushing and James D. Laing. *Organizational Evaluation and Authority,* Technical Report No. 17. Stanford: Stanford University, Laboratory for Social Research, 1966.

Sewell, William, Archie O. Haller and Murray A. Straus. "Social Status and Educational and Occupational Aspiration," *American Sociological Review,* XII, No. 1 (1957), 67-73.

Singleton, Robert, and Paul Bullock. "Some Problems in Minority-Group Education in Los Angeles Public Schools," *Journal of Negro Education,* XXXII, No. 2 (1963), 137-145.

Sprey, Jetse. "Sex Differences in Occupational Choice Patterns Among Negro Adolescents," *Social Forces,* XLI, No. 1 (1962), 11-23.

Stephenson, R. M. "Mobility Orientation and Stratification of 1,000 Ninth Graders," *American Sociological Review,* XXII, No. 1 (1957), 67-73.

Stinchcombe, Arthur. *Rebellion in a High School,* Chicago, Ill.: Quadrangle Books Inc., 1964.

Tannenbaum, Abraham. "Curriculum Perspectives for Slum Schools," *The High School and the Big Cities: Conference Report,* N. Boyan (ed.), 1-3. Mimeo Conference Report, Stanford University, 1963.

Thomas, L. "Prospects of Scientific Research into Values," *Educational Theory,* 6 (1956), 193-214.

Wallin, Paul, and Leslie Waldo. *Social Class Background of 8th Grade Pupils, Social Class Composition of Their Schools, Their Academic Aspirations and School Adjustment,* Cooperative Research Project No. 1935. Stanford University, 1964.

Wilson, Alan B. "Educational Consequences of Segregation in a California Community," *Appendices: Racial Isolation in the Public Schools,* II. Washington: U.S. Government Printing Office, Commission on Civil Rights, 1967, pp. 165-206.

Wilson, Alan B. "Residential Segregation of Social Classes and Aspirations of High School Boys," *American Sociological Review,* XXIV, No. 6 (1959), 836-845.

Wolff, Max. "Segregation in the Schools of Gary, Indiana," *Journal of Educational Sociology,* XXXVI, No. 6 (1963), 251-261.

Wolfle, Dael. "Editorial," *Science,* CLVI (April 7, 1967), 19.

INDEX